W9-AMS-135

English Romanticism

English Romanticism

Laura K. Egendorf, *Book Editor*

David L. Bender, *Publisher*

Bruno Leone, *Executive Editor*

Bonnie Szumski, *Editorial Director*

Stuart B. Miller, *Managing Editor*

David M. Haugen, *Series Editor*

Greenhaven Press, Inc., San Diego, CA

Every effort has been made to trace the owners of copy-
righted material. The articles in this volume may have
been edited for content, length, and/or reading level. The
titles have been changed to enhance the editorial purpose.
Those interested in locating the original source will find
the complete citation on the first page of each article.

Library of Congress Cataloging-in-Publication Data

English romanticism / Laura K. Egendorf.
        p. cm. — (Greenhaven Press companion to literary
movements and genres)
    Includes bibliographical references and index.
    ISBN 0-7377-0570-1 (lib. bdg.) —
ISBN 0-7377-0569-8 (pbk. : alk. paper)
    1. English literature—18th century—History and
criticism. 2. English literature—19th century—History
and criticism. 3. Romanticism–Great Britain. I. Egendorf,
Laura K., 1973–   . II. Series.

PR447 .E58 2001
820.9'145—dc21

00-046233
CIP

Cover photo: Tate Gallery/Art Resource
Library of Congress, 36, 64, 72, 118, 132
North Wind Picture Archives, 87

Copyright © 2001 by Greenhaven Press, Inc.
PO Box 289009
San Diego, CA 92198-9009
Printed in the U.S.A.

CONTENTS

Chapter 1: The Elements of English Romanticism

Romanticism was a reaction to the Classicism movement,
which had desired reason and objectivity. As a result, key
characteristics of Romantic literature are imagination and
an escape from the constrictions of modern life.

For the Romantics, imagination was a powerful force that
could unite man with nature and was a central element to
their poetry and philosophy. The Romantics embraced
imagination as a response to the sterile and mechanistic
philosophies that were common in the eighteenth century.

Nature was important to the Romantics. Their poems and
novels reflect the belief that natural scenery was a source of
intense feelings and moral inspiration. The Romantics also
believed that man should try to be in harmony with nature.

Eighteenth-century Romantic lyrics—short poems that express personal emotion—place considerable emphasis on
meditation. The meditative quality associated with the
lyric typifies the Romantic poems, but is actually a device
borrowed from metaphysical poems and local poems of
the previous century.

Romantic poets were helped and hindered by efforts to explain religion in their works. For many of these poets, religion was self-deifying—they tended to worship themselves
as much as any god.

Chapter 2: The Romantic Poets

Scott's interest in wilderness and the supernatural links him with his contemporaries. However, the title character also exhibits detrimental Romantic qualities, such as an impressionable nature, that can lead to trouble or ruin.

Chapter 4: Critiquing the Movement

FOREWORD

The study of literature most often involves focusing on an individual work and uncovering its themes, stylistic conventions, and historical relevance. It is also enlightening to examine multiple works by a single author, identifying similarities and differences among texts and tracing the author's development as an artist.

While the study of individual works and authors is instructive, however, examining groups of authors who shared certain cultural or historical experiences adds a further richness to the study of literature. By focusing on literary movements and genres, readers gain a greater appreciation of influence of historical events and social circumstances on the development of particular literary forms and themes. For example, in the early twentieth century, rapid technological and industrial advances, mass urban migration, World War I, and other events contributed to the emergence of a movement known as American modernism. The dramatic social changes, and the uncertainty they created, were reflected in an increased use of free verse in poetry, the stream-of-consciousness technique in fiction, and a general sense of historical discontinuity and crisis of faith in most of the literature of the era. By focusing on these commonalities, readers attain a more comprehensive picture of the complex interplay of social, economic, political, aesthetic, and philosophical forces and ideas that create the tenor of any era. In the nineteenth-century American romanticism movement, for example, authors shared many ideas concerning the preeminence of the self-reliant individual, the infusion of nature with spiritual significance, and the potential of persons to achieve transcendence via communion with nature. However, despite their commonalities, American romantics often differed significantly in their thematic and stylistic approaches. Walt Whitman celebrated the communal nature of America's open democratic society, while Ralph Waldo

Emerson expressed the need for individuals to pursue their own fulfillment regardless of their fellow citizens. Herman Melville wrote novels in a largely naturalistic style whereas Nathaniel Hawthorne's novels were gothic and allegorical.

Another valuable reason to investigate literary movements and genres lies in their potential to clarify the process of literary evolution. By examining groups of authors, literary trends across time become evident. The reader learns, for instance, how English romanticism was transformed as it crossed the Atlantic to America. The poetry of Lord Byron, William Wordsworth, and John Keats celebrated the restorative potential of rural scenes. The American romantics, writing later in the century, shared their English counterparts' faith in nature; but American authors were more likely to present an ambiguous view of nature as a source of liberation as well as the dwelling place of personal demons. The whale in Melville's *Moby-Dick* and the forests in Hawthorne's novels and stories bear little resemblance to the benign pastoral scenes in Wordsworth's lyric poems.

Each volume in Greenhaven Press's Companions to Literary Movements and Genres series begins with an introductory essay that places the topic in a historical and literary context. The essays that follow are carefully chosen and edited for ease of comprehension. These essays are arranged into clearly defined chapters that are outlined in a concise annotated table of contents. Finally, a thorough chronology maps out crucial literary milestones of the movement or genre as well as significant social and historical events. Readers will benefit from the structure and coherence that these features lend to material that is often challenging. With Greenhaven's Literary Movements and Genres in hand, readers will be better able to comprehend and appreciate the major literary works and their impact on society.

INTRODUCTION

Few images in literature evoke as much terror as that of Victor Frankenstein bringing his monster to life. It is an image that has been depicted in many film adaptations, ranging from movies that hew closely to Mary Shelley's novel to those that are largely parody. Her book, written in 1817, is but one example of how English Romanticism has remained influential, nearly two centuries after its peak.

One reason Romanticism is still appealing is its emphasis on universal concepts that have remained important, such as revolution, imagination, and the power of the individual. Romanticism was revolutionary because it advocated change; for example, many of the Romantics supported the goals of the French Revolution because of its inherent promise to abolish monarchy and bring about social reform. Closely linked to the revolutionary spirit was the Romantics' trust in imagination. Through this gift the Romantics could dream of a better world, one that was not constrained by the rational paradigms of the Enlightenment that were so closely linked to the past—to the status quo. Lastly, the Romantics emphasized individualism, a belief that people's lives could be epic and foster change if put to the test.

Of course, all these beliefs that these writers held came through in their works. William Wordsworth's "The Prelude" is a deeply autobiographical poem that exults in the power of nature and imagination. Lord Byron's tempestuous, larger-than-life lifestyle was reflected in Childe Harold and Manfred, characters who fight undaunted against forces that seek to restrain them. Those Byronic heroes would be echoed in later characters such as Heathcliff, from Emily Bronte's novel *Wuthering Heights*, and Captain Ahab, from Herman Melville's novel *Moby-Dick*.

While the characters who filled these Romantic poems and novels were often larger than life, their creators were frequently more interesting. They held ideas about religion and society that many of their contemporaries would find alarming; for example, William Blake believed that divinity could be found within man. In general, the novelists were more temperate than the poets, although Mary Wollstonecraft Godwin succeeded in shocking her father, William Godwin, by eloping with the married Percy Bysshe Shelley. But of all these authors, Byron was the most controversial. He had gained almost instant fame upon the publication of "Childe Harold" in 1812, but in the next twelve years would become nearly as famous for his amorous scandals and adventurous lifestyle as he would for his poetry. Today the views and actions of these men would probably not be at all shocking, but in the late eighteenth and early nineteenth centuries, the Romantics stood sharply against the literary and social values of their time.

THE ART REMAINS VITAL

The radical views and personal foibles of the English Romantics have long since passed into history, but their poems and novels remain eternal. "La Belle Dame Sans Merci," by John Keats, "Ozymandias" by Percy Bysshe Shelley, and "The Tables Turned," by Wordsworth, and the Romantic novels of Sir Walter Scott, are perennials in high school and college literature courses. Not all of the Romantics have remained as relevant as these men—for example, few people are still studying the works of Southey, who was lambasted in his own time by Byron. However, poets such as Blake, Wordsworth, Samuel Taylor Coleridge, Byron, Shelley, and John Keats, along with various Romantic novelists and essayists, have yet to wear out their welcome.

This volume explores the key themes and characteristics of some of the most important works in English Romanticism. By providing a gamut of views by many prominent Romantic scholars, the editor hopes that the modern reader will join the countless others who have been inspired by the powerful imagery and intense feelings that mark the literature of the Romantic era.

ENGLISH ROMANTICISM: AN OVERVIEW

The fifty-year span from 1780 to 1830 was a time of great turmoil in England and the rest of Europe. England went to war against its maturing North American colonies; first, as those colonies sought independence and again in 1812 over other political and economic issues. France would undergo two revolutions and the rule of Napoléon in just that half-century, while other European countries, among them Ireland and Belgium, also faced revolution and dissent. The revolutionary aspects of that epoch were reflected not only in political unrest but also in a new current of literature. That literature is known as Romanticism, a style that swept Europe during the late eighteenth and early nineteenth centuries.

The English Romantics are the creators of some of the era's greatest works; their writings reflected in many ways the revolutionary feelings that were sweeping Europe. For these writers—notably William Blake, Percy Bysshe Shelley, and Walter Scott—the revolutions (especially those in France) were a source of both delight and concern. To some of these writers, particularly Shelley, the French Revolution was a powerful and inspiring cataclysm. However, other Romantics had a more conservative view of revolution and advocated a more pastoral, domestic life. The revolutionary aspects of English Romanticism were inspired by more than the political situation, however; these poets, essayists, and novelists also formed a literary and social revolution, as they rose up against the neoclassicism and social mores of the mid-1700s.

THE IMPORTANCE OF THE FRENCH REVOLUTION

Before examining the literary influences on the Romantics, it is necessary to consider perhaps the most important political influence—the French Revolution. Few historical events have had a greater impact than the uprising that began in 1789. As noted historian E.J. Hobsbawm states in his book *The Age of Revolution: 1789–1848*:

> The French Revolution may not have been an isolated phe-
> nomenon, but it was far more fundamental than any of the
> other contemporary ones and its consequences were there-
> fore far more profound. In the first place, it occurred in the
> most powerful and populous state of Europe (leaving Russia
> apart). In 1789 something like one European out of every five
> was a Frenchman. In the second place it was, alone of all the
> revolutions which preceded and followed it, a mass *social*
> revolution, and immeasurably more radical than any compa-
> rable upheaval.[1]

For the first few heady years of the French Revolution, from the events of 1789—the meeting of the National Assembly (merchants, artisans, peasants, and professional men and some members of the nobility and clergy) from May to June and the fall of the Bastille prison on July 14, 1789—until September 1792, when the monarchy was abolished, it seemed to many people inside and outside France that the Revolution was a justified overturning of oppressive rule. Yet upheaval did not bring peace, as violence and factionalizing took hold, eventually leading to the Reign of Terror, in which seventeen thousand people—including many of the leading revolutionaries—were executed in fourteen months. In the early years, however, the Revolution and the unbridled optimism of its calls for liberty and equality for the middle class and peasantry inspired many poets and novelists. The French constitution was approved in 1791 and the nobility abolished in favor of a constitutional monarchy. The most important section of the constitution was the Declaration of the Rights of Man, which made all Frenchmen equal in the eyes of the law and gave them the right to vote and the right to free speech.

Some of the greatest poets and thinkers of the time supported the French Revolution—at least in its early years—including the French philosopher Jean-Jacques Rousseau. Among the prominent German proponents were the philosopher Immanuel Kant and the poet Friedrich von Schiller. Blake and William Wordsworth also looked hopefully on the French Revolution, as several of their poems indicate. In his autobiographical poem "The Prelude," Wordsworth wrote favorably of his travels in France from 1791 to 1792. According to Heather Coombs, in her book *The Age of Keats and Shelley:*

"To Wordsworth, and to many of his contemporaries, the French Revolution seemed at first to be not so much a historical event as a turning-point in the existence of man, the start of an ideal civilization."[2] In 1791, Blake wrote "The French Revolution," an epic poem that recounts the early days of the Revolution and condemns social and political tyranny.

MEDIEVAL INFLUENCES ON ENGLISH ROMANTICISM

The French Revolution would prove to have a significant effect on the works of both the first and second generation of Romantics. However, these writers were inspired not only by the world that surrounded them, but by their predecessors in medieval society and literature. To the Romantics, the stories of days gone by were vastly preferable to the uninspiring intellect of the neoclassical age in which they were living. In the introduction to his book *The Beginnings of the English Romantic Movement*, William Lyon Phelps, who had been a professor of English at Yale University, observed:

> In the Middle Age lay just the material for which the Romantic spirit yearned. Its religious, military and social life and all forms of mediaeval art can hardly be better characterized than by the word *Picturesque*; and souls weary of form and finish, of "dead perfection," of "faultily faultless" monotony, naturally sought the opposite of all this in literature and thought of the Middle Ages.[3]

Among the poems and novels set during the Middle Ages were Samuel Taylor Coleridge's "Christabel," Scott's *Ivanhoe*, and John Keats's "The Eve of St. Agnes" and "La Belle Dame Sans Merci." The latter poem showed perhaps the greatest medieval influence. Keats's portrayal of knights and mysterious fairies echoed similar medieval tales, and it shared its title with a medieval poem by Alain Chartier. Keats's medieval proclivities were also influenced by Edmund Spenser and his most famous work, *The Faerie Queene*.

LOCAL AND METAPHYSICAL POEMS

Another influence on the Romantics, in particular Coleridge, were two types of poems common in the seventeenth and eighteenth centuries: local poems and metaphysical poems. Local poems were named for specific geographical locations and combined a description of the location with expression of the poet's thoughts and feelings while observing the scenery. The Romantics would follow suit with poems such as Wordsworth's "Lines Composed a Few Miles Above Tintern Abbey" and Coleridge's "This Lime-Tree Bower My Prison." In these poems, the authors combined descriptions of scenery with the personal impressions inspired by such scenes. Metaphysical poems, common in the seventeenth century, did not describe specific scenery, but their emphasis on meditation on spiritual crises can be seen in Romantic works by Coleridge and Shelley, in particular.

Although the devotional and local poems were not Romantic, books that could be considered Romantic were being written as early as the 1750s. These works consisted largely of literary criticism, rather than poetry itself; their authors urged poets to turn away from the classical style so admired by Renaissance writers and scholars and instead look toward nature for inspiration.

REACTING AGAINST THE NEOCLASSICISTS

However, Romantic poetry might have been shaped most not by earlier poems, but by the society in which the Romantics lived. In particular, the Romantics shunned the writing and thinking of the late eighteenth century that was known as neoclassicism. In general, the Romantics found mechanistic science and materialism worthy of disdain and lacking inspiration.

In contrast, the Romantics' interest lay in nature, emotions, and imagination. They wanted to break loose from the chains of modern society and explore the idealized worlds that they created in their mind. R.B. Mowat, a professor of history at the University of Bristol in England, writes: "In literature Romanticism is contrasted with classicism—with the school of thought which attached value to form, rule, precision, symmetry, repose. The Romantic movement represented an intellectual revolt of the younger generation against convention."[4] Blake's poetry, in particular "Jerusalem" and "Milton," best showed these views. Mark Richard Barna notes that Blake rejected the predominant beliefs of England during the Age of Reason. Also known as the Enlightenment, the Age of Reason was a current of thinking in the eighteenth century that emphasized rationality, science, and secularism over religion. Three great seventeenth-century thinkers served as inspiration to the Enlightenment: mathematician and scientist Isaac Newton and the philosophers Francis Bacon and John Locke, who shared with Newton a deep interest in science.

And yet, while Blake turned against the Age of Reason, not all of his peers rejected eighteenth-century thought. Although some thinkers of that era were scorned, many of the great minds of the Enlightenment did inspire the Romantics. The chief tenet of the Enlightenment was the power of human reason and the corollary belief that through experience and observation, humans could learn and change for the better. For the Romantics, the most influential of the Enlightenment thinkers was most likely Rousseau, whose works *Confession, Emile,* and *The Social Contract* made their mark on educational and political theories. Another important Enlightenment figure was Thomas Paine, an ardent supporter of the American and French Revolutions. His seminal work, *The Rights of Man,* would spark the reply of Mary Wollstonecraft's 1792 treatise, *Vindication of the Rights of Women.* Wollstonecraft and her husband, fellow writer and philosopher William Godwin, would prove to be important figures in the Romantic movement. Their daughter, Mary Wollstonecraft Godwin (whose birth led to infection and death for the elder Mary) would grow up to become Mary Shelley, wife of Percy Bysshe and the author of *Frankenstein.* In fact, the Shelleys' courtship grew out of Percy Shelley's adoration for Godwin's writing and his subsequent visits to Godwin's home. Like other Enlightenment figures, Godwin, Wollstonecraft, and Paine were also admired by the Romantics for their support of the French Revolution.

THE EARLY ROMANTIC POETS

With this overview of key influences on the English Romantics in mind, the best way to understand the movement is by studying the lives and works of the major writers. Blake, Wordsworth, and Coleridge are considered by most literary scholars to be the poets who led the first wave of English Romanticism. All three were supporters of the French Revolution, but as time passed and the Reign of Terror swept through France, they began to seek new inspiration. What had seemed like a promising revolution would ultimately fail. By 1799 France would be ruled by the autocratic Napoléon I, who would declare himself emperor five years later. Disillusioned, Blake, Wordsworth, and Coleridge turned their attention in other directions.

The power of the imagination became William Blake's focus. As James Engell, a professor of English and comparative literature at Harvard University, explains: "Blake champions the freedom of the creative mind and has no doubts what purpose that freedom should serve. The imaginative life is the only real life."[5] To Blake, imagination was a transforming force. Imagination was central to Romanticism, and Blake showed why in his poetry, which emphasized the belief that the human mind could create a more perfect world.

As with imagination and revolution, nature was important to the Romantics. Karl Kroeber, a professor of humanities at Columbia University, writes:

> An enormous number of romantic poems focus on . . . how to retain self-reverence even while skeptically scrutinizing our impulses and motivations, since we are all adept at self-betrayal. The fundamental solution is suggested by . . . Wordsworth: recognize oneself not as an isolated being but as one fully existent only insofar as reciprocally interacting with one's environment. . . . Implicit in this view is a powerful if unusual politics: the most trivial, commonplace, unnoticed of persons is naturally deserving of respect as an individual. That is *the* fundamental romantic political commitment. It is founded on the conviction that we are not alienated, unless through morbid narcissism we alienate ourselves and lose the wealth of gentle sensations to be experienced in process of full reciprocity with our natural habitat.[6]

William Wordsworth and Samuel Taylor Coleridge are especially remembered for their interest in nature. The two men, who were close friends and the coauthors of *Lyrical Ballads,* are known for their poems that concerned their experiences with nature and the ways in which nature is a source of knowledge and beauty. As Wordsworth famously puts it in "The Tables Turned":

> One impulse from a vernal wood
> May teach you more of man,
> Of moral evil and of good,
> Than all the sages can.[7]

Coleridge echoes similar thoughts in "Frost at Midnight," a poem written for his son. Coleridge tells his son that he will be raised among nature:

> . . . *thou,* my babe! shalt wander like the breeze
> By lakes and sandy shores, beneath the crags
> Of ancient mountain, . . .
> so shalt thou see and hear
> The lovely shapes and sounds intelligible
> Of that eternal language.[8]

THE LATER ROMANTIC POETS

The next wave of Romantic poets—Byron, Shelley, and Keats—would also express their love of nature in poems such as Shelley's "Ode to the West Wind" and Keats's "Ode to a Nightingale." However, these men, Byron and Shelley in particular, were even more committed to revolutionary ideals than their predecessors, despite the fact that Byron was a small child and Shelley not yet born when the French Revolution was at its height. Byron and Shelley's personal lives were a form of rebellion as well, standing in opposition to English society.

Lord Byron would in fact die in the course of a revolution. He traveled to Greece to support that nation's revolt against Turkey and died of a fever in 1824 in Missolonghi, Greece. In his poetry and his life, Byron scoffed at traditional values. He wed once, but abandoned his wife and daughter not long after the child's birth; had an illegitimate child with Claire Clairmont, the stepsister of Mary Shelley; and was known for his dalliances with men and women. Although he was a member of the English peerage, Byron spent his adult life on the Continent, where he befriended fellow expatriates, most notably the Shelleys and Leigh Hunt. His most famous works are about similarly rakish and rebellious men, since known as "Byronic heroes." These characters—Manfred, Childe Harold, Cain, and Don Juan—have committed grave sins, and though they feel remorse, they continue to live proudly and defiantly. Don Juan is the most humorous of these heroes, while Manfred, whose sin is incest, best exemplifies the Byronic hero's refusal to bow to traditional mores and beliefs. He dies at the end of the poem, having rejected an abbot's wishes to reconcile Manfred with the church. Instead, Manfred faces death with defiance, unafraid of the demons who have come for his soul or what he might face in the afterlife: "Old man! 'tis not so difficult to die."[9] Leslie A. Marchand, the author of *Byron's Poetry*, notes that Manfred's expressions of his belief in his immortal spirit and unconquerable mind can be seen as overly egotistical but concludes: "From another point of view Byron's statements of intransigent human longings and despair must remain a poetic landmark of the romantic agony."[10]

While the older Romantics began to question the outcome of the French Revolution, Percy Bysshe Shelley remained an ardent supporter of the cause. Notes Coombs: "We have proof in the poetry of Shelley that the French Revolution still seemed, in spite of its failure, to be a great example of a struggle for liberty, and a powerful portent of what man could achieve."[11] Shelley was staunchly against the monarchy—as was Keats—and in addition to his poetry, Shelley also wrote political pamphlets. Although Shelley was deeply affected by the French Revolution, he believed that it failed because its leaders began to depend too much on the use of violence. His poem "The Revolt of Islam" depicts a bloodless and successful revolution that he believed was a possible alternative to the violence of the Reign of Terror. He also supported the Greek revolt against Turkey and wrote in praise of Greece in "Hellas." As was the case with Byron, Shelley turned away from English upper-class morality. He eloped with Mary Godwin in summer 1814, leaving his first wife, Harriet; divorce in England was nearly impossible at the time, and the couple could not wed until December 1816, following Harriet's suicide. The Shelleys would travel throughout Europe, living primarily in Italy and Switzerland, until 1822, when Shelley drowned when the boat he and a friend were trying to sail from Livorno to Le Spezia, Italy, capsized.

John Keats was not as revolutionary-minded as his compatriots, but he did share Shelley's belief that a better society could be built. However, Coombs observes that Keats sought to create a better place not by overt action but by bringing beauty into the world. She writes: "Keats' way of '*benefiting*' the world, then, is to concentrate upon what he calls '*the principle of beauty in all things.*'"[12] One poem that exemplifies these views is "Ode to Psyche," in which Keats pledges to the goddess that he will bring her beauty and message to everyone:

> So let me be thy choir, and make a moan
> > Upon the midnight hours;
> Thy voice, thy lute, thy pipe, thy incense sweet
> > From swinged censer teeming;
> Thy shrine, thy grove, thy oracle, thy heat
> > Of pale-mouthed prophet dreaming.[13]

THE ROMANTIC NOVELISTS

While the Romantic period is chiefly associated with poetry, the era also nurtured the careers of preeminent novelists and essayists. In general, the Romantic qualities of these writers were not as prominent as they were for the poets. For example, Jane Austen ignored political issues in her novels—military characters figure prominently in many of her works, most particularly *Persuasion* (generally considered her most Romantic novel), but Austen does not explicitly refer to the battles between England and France that took place during the early nineteenth century.

Mary Shelley is an especially interesting case. For a woman who was the progeny of two of the best minds of the eighteenth century and the wife of one of the great Romantic poets, Mary Shelley was not as hopeful about the power of the human mind as one might expect. She was an example of the feminine Romantic. Some literary critics have noted that female Romantic writers were not as interested in revolution and creating new worlds as they were in improving the existing community and domestic relations. The unfortunate social reality was that women authors could not present ideas as radical as those of their male counterparts. Literary scholar Julie Shaffer writes: "The formal and social requirements accepted as obtaining on the era's female novelists have been seen as forcing them to write works ultimately conservative in most senses, and certainly so in terms of the attacks on the class system ostensibly offered by canonical Romanticism."[14] Domestic relations and the role of men and women are central to Mary Shelley's novel *Frankenstein: Or, the Modern Prometheus.* She describes the tragedy that results when Victor Frankenstein usurps the female role of mother by building his monster and then, unlike a devoted mother, rejecting his "child," which leads to the murders of those Frankenstein loves most and his own death. The title of her novel refers to the mythical figure Prometheus, who in Greek mythology was punished by the god Zeus for having given fire to mankind. Later myths say that Prometheus created humans. In Mary Shelley's hands, the ability to create can be dangerous; she distrusts the possibilities of science. In contrast, Percy Shelley had always been entranced by scientific experiments; and in his poem "Prometheus Unbound," written several years after his wife's novel, the title character is more heroic and the poem ends on a happy note.

Sir Walter Scott also blended Romantic and anti-Romantic attitudes in his works. Scott's novels often dealt with the issues of revolution and rebellion, but from a historical perspective. Rather than write about the French Revolution, Scott wrote novels about the Jacobite Rebellion. The Jacobites were people in England and Scotland who sought to return the Stuart dynasty, which had been dethroned by William of Orange during the Glorious Revolution of 1688, to its rightful place in the monarchy. They named themselves after King James II, whose Latin name was Jacob. The Jacobites led two unsuccessful rebellions in their effort to have James's son, and later his grandson, crowned king, the first in 1715, the second in 1745 (known as "The Forty-Five"). The latter rebellion formed the plot of Scott's novel *Waverley*, whose title character becomes involved in "The Forty-Five." However, Scott is not wholly supportive of the rebellion nor is he as interested as Shelley or Byron in creating a heroic figure. For Scott, there is such a thing as striving to be too Romantic or too heroic. During the course of the novel, Waverley begins to question the goals and efforts of the Jacobite cause. At the conclusion of *Waverley*, he is a married, wealthy landowner who has become reconciled to the existing government. Despite these criticisms of revolutionary behavior, Scott was a Romantic in many ways, especially in the evocative power of nature and landscapes in his novels.

Of the essayists and novelists, William Hazlitt was probably the most devoted to the Romantic cause. Author and literary critic Harold Bloom writes: "William Hazlitt . . . kept his faith in the Revolution and even in Napoleon long after every other literary figure of the time had turned reactionary or indifferent, or had died young. . . . His entire background and career are archetypal of English Romanticism."[15] Hazlitt's interest in revolution is not surprising, as his father supported the American colonies' fight for independence and the family lived in America during part of Hazlitt's childhood. Hazlitt was also an admirer of the French writers like Rousseau.

FRENCH AND GERMAN ROMANTICISM

Although the focus of these pages is the English Romantics, Romanticism was an important literary movement throughout Europe. Toward the end of the eighteenth century, some German writers began to reject the neoclassical style, emphasizing instead nature, revolution, and youthful rebellion. Their new style, Sturm und Drang ("Storm and Stress"), was a precursor to Romanticism. One of the most famous works of the Sturm und Drang movement is Johann von Goethe's 1774 novel, *The Sorrows of Young Werther*, which told the story of a young man who commits suicide after he experiences a failed relationship. By the early years of the nineteenth century, a Romantic school had formed in Berlin. Among its leaders were the brothers August Wilhelm and Friedrich Schlegel and the poet Friedrich Leopold, who wrote under the pen name Novalis. Like Keats and Coleridge, Novalis looked to the Middle Ages for inspiration. Other key German Romantics included Heinrich Heine and the Brothers Grimm. Their works featured cosmopolitan, often semiautobiographical heroes, a love of nature, and an emphasis on solitariness and melancholy.

As inspirational as the French Revolution was to the English Romantics, it can come as no surprise that literature of France also changed after 1789. French writers such as Constantin-François Volney and the marquis de Condorcet had praised the Revolution and expressed their belief that the events in France were proof that mankind could perfect itself and establish a utopian society. As was the case in England, French Romanticism was also interested in expressing powerful emotions.

THE DECLINE OF ROMANTICISM

By 1830, Europe had gone through many dramatic changes. France had experienced imperial rule under Napoléon I, whose power ended with his defeat by British and Prussian armies at Waterloo in 1815. In his place came the return of the Bourbons, the royal house that had previously ruled France for two centuries. Fifteen years later, France experienced another revolution in barely four decades. That revolution would lead to the establishment of a constitutional monarchy, led by Louis Philippe, who was also from the Bourbon line. As was typical for France during that era, yet another revolution would follow and in 1848, Louis Philippe would fall.

Although England did not experience the near-continual turmoil of France, many important changes did occur. In less than fifty years, the nation would have four monarchs. King George III began to suffer bouts of madness, brought on by porphyria, as early as 1789; in 1811 he was declared insane and his son, the Prince of Wales, was named regent. Nine years later, George III died and his son became King

George IV. His reign lasted only ten years, and his brother, King William IV, succeeded him on his death. William's brief reign included the passage of the Reform Act in 1832. That act extended the vote to an additional 500,000 citizens and provided for a more equitable distribution of parliamentary seats. A mass social movement also began to develop among the British working poor. Britain was taking on a new form, transforming from a largely agricultural society into an industrial nation. In 1837, William would die childless, succeeded by his niece Victoria.

By this time, English Romanticism had largely run its course. England had grown increasingly conservative and the ideals of Romanticism were no longer in vogue. Victoria's ascension to the throne had been preceded by the deaths of Blake, Byron, Shelley, Keats, Hazlitt, Austen, Scott, Coleridge, and Charles Lamb. The Romantics who survived no longer held their earlier, revolutionary views. Wordsworth, who had at first ardently supported the French Revolution, was repulsed by its growing violence and became increasingly conservative. In 1843, he was considered respectable enough to be named poet laureate of England, a post he held until his death in 1850. Other prominent Romantics, including Coleridge and Thomas Carlyle, would also begin to express more conservative views in their works. However, for the most part their careers had ended during the reign of William IV. Wordsworth did release a book of poetry in 1835, and Carlyle would write a biography of Walter Scott and *Sartor Resartus*, a work that combined a novel, essays, and autobiography, in the 1830s. Coleridge's output ended even before then. Although two of his later works—*Biographia Literaria*, a work of literary criticism published in 1817, and 1825's *Aids to Reflection*, a religious and philosophical treatise—were considered among his finest, Coleridge had written little poetry since the early nineteenth century.

THE LEGACY OF ROMANTICISM

Romanticism did not die completely, however. Even in staid Victorian times, some poets exhibited Romantic qualities. Shelley was an influence on the early work of Robert Browning, who used Shelleyan imagery such as caves and serpents in the poem "Pauline." Both Shelley and Keats influenced Alfred Tennyson; like Keats, Tennyson set several of his works in the Middle Ages, most famously his Arthurian poems. The influence of Keats would lead to the formation in the mid–nineteenth century of the Pre-Raphaelite school, whose members included Dante Gabriel Rossetti and William Holman Hunt. Coombs writes: "The Pre-Raphaelites felt strongly the link between painting and literature, and . . . they frequently turned to literature which was either really of a bygone age—for example Dante or Shakespeare—or more contemporary writers who depicted medieval scenes, such as Keats (occasionally Byron) and Tennyson."[16] Wordsworth influenced the works of John Ruskin—who, like Wordsworth, sought morals within nature—and William Butler Yeats, among others. The Brontë sisters would center novels around characters who have been labeled Byronic heroes—Heathcliff in Emily's *Wuthering Heights* and Rochester in Charlotte's *Jane Eyre*. However, argues Kenneth Allott, a professor of English at the University of Liverpool prior to his death in 1973, the Victorian-era poets could not be wholly Romantic, in the context of the expectations and desires of the society in which they lived. The Victorian era was a time of rapid social change that left the urban working class in considerable strife and poverty. Rather than mimic the Romantic writers and their emphasis on nature and imagination, many Victorian authors turned to realistic depictions of life and wrote novels that expressed their opinions on issues such as the Industrial Revolution and class inequalities. Allott also notes: "Their poetry is Romantic poetry, but it differs from the greatest Romantics in having to serve two masters: the individually mediated and almost private vision of truth—the truth of the imagination; and the social 'truth' of the marketplace, which as good Victorians themselves, the poets did not feel they could ignore."[17] In the Victorian marketplace, reason and realism—present in the novels of Charles Dickens, for example—are what appealed most to the middle class.

Despite the many political, economic, and social changes that have occurred since the height of the Romantic era, its poetry has remained important long after its last writer died. As Harold Bloom and Lionel Trilling write in their introduction to *Romantic Poetry and Prose*: "Recurrent romanticism is apparently endemic in human nature; all men and women are questers to some degree. . . . The literature of internalized quest, of Promethean aspiration, is the most vitalizing and formidable achievement in the Western arts since the Renaissance."[18]

NOTES

1. E.J. Hobsbawm, *The Age of Revolution: 1789–1848.* New York: Mentor, 1962, p. 75.

2. Heather Coombs, *The Age of Keats and Shelley.* London: Blackie, 1978, p. 41.

3. William Lyon Phelps, *The Beginnings of the English Romantic Movement.* Boston: Ginn, 1893, p. 5.

4. R.B. Mowat, *The Romantic Age: Europe in the Early Nineteenth Century.* London: George G. Harrap, 1937, p. 48.

5. James Engell, *The Creative Imagination: Enlightenment to Romanticism.* Cambridge, MA: Harvard University Press, 1981, p. 244.

6. Karl Kroeber, *Ecological Literary Criticism: Romantic Imagining and the Biology of Mind.* New York: Columbia University Press, 1994, p. 70.

7. William Wordsworth, "The Tables Turned," ll. 21–24.

8. Samuel Taylor Coleridge, "Frost at Midnight," ll. 54–60.

9. Lord Byron, "Manfred," act 3, scene 4, l. 151.

10. Leslie A. Marchand, *Byron's Poetry: A Critical Introduction.* Boston: Houghton Mifflin, 1965, p. 84.

11. Coombs, *The Age of Keats and Shelley,* p. 42.

12. Coombs, *The Age of Keats and Shelley,* p. 64.

13. John Keats, "Ode to Psyche," ll. 44–49.

14. Julie Shaffer, "Non-Canonical Women's Novels of the Romantic Era: Romantic Ideologies and the Problematics of Gender and Genre," *Studies in the Novel,* Winter 1996, p. 473.

15. Harold Bloom, *The Visionary Company: A Reading of English Romantic Poetry.* Ithaca, NY: Cornell University Press, 1971, p. xvii.

16. Coombs, *The Age of Keats and Shelley,* p. 175.

17. Kenneth Allott, "Victorian Poetry and the Legacy of Romanticism," in R.T. Davies and B.G. Beatty, eds., *Literature of the Romantic Period: 1750–1850.* Liverpool, England: Liverpool University Press, 1976, p. 200.

18. Harold Bloom and Lionel Trilling, eds., *The Oxford Anthology of English Literature: Romantic Poetry and Prose.* New York: Oxford University Press, 1973, p. 9.

CHAPTER 1

The Elements of English Romanticism

English
Romanticism

General Characteristics of Romantic Literature

Thomas McFarland

Thomas McFarland provides an overview of some of the central elements of Romantic literature. According to McFarland, the authors and philosophers of the genre were interested in juxtaposing themselves against Classicism, which emphasized reason and objectivity. Consequently, the Romantics sought to escape from ordered reality by writing highly subjective works that relied heavily on the imagination. Exotic locales and dreamscapes became the settings for poems and novels that dealt with supernatural encounters or other events outside the realm of everyday experience. Romanticism offered freedom from old conventions and came to symbolize the major political and social changes taking place throughout Europe. McFarland has written several books on Romanticism, including *Romanticism and the Heritage of Rousseau* and *Romantic Cruxes: The English Essayists and the Spirit of the Age*, from which the following article is excerpted.

Exactly what Romanticism is has been scarcely agreed upon by commentators, though it is possible to list many of its characteristics. These are often most tellingly juxtaposed against the predecessor sensibility referred to as neoclassicism. Romanticism celebrates external nature ('For what has made the sage or poet write?', asks [John] Keats, 'But the fair paradise of Nature's light'), which constituted a reaction against neoclassicism's love of the city and the ideal of human, not external nature. Classicism held up as its ideal the sun of Reason, while Romanticism took refuge in the moonlit realms of Imagination. Classicism satirized the vagaries of the individual ego; Romanticism hailed Rousseauistic subjectivity and Byronic egotism.[1] Classicism sought for the general: 'Great thoughts are always general,' wrote Dr. [Samuel] Johnson, 'and consist in positions not limited by exceptions, and in descriptions not descending to minuteness.' Romanticism on the contrary hailed the particular: 'Singular & Particular Detail is the Foundation of the Sublime', wrote [William] Blake. 'To Generalize is to be an Idiot. To Particularize is the Alone Distinction of Merit.'

THE INFLUENCE OF THE MEDIEVAL AND ORIENTAL

Other emphases of Romanticism, besides external nature, imagination, egotism, and love of the particular, centre upon a protean variety of flights from reality: into the exotic world of medieval imagining, into the radically other world of visionary oriental setting, into the world of dreams, into drugs. Of these, the imaginative reconstruction of the middle ages took special pride of place. 'What was the Romantic School in Germany?' asked Heine in a famous question, to which he readily supplied an equally famous answer: 'It was nothing other than the reawakening of the poetry of the middle ages, as it manifested itself in the poems, paintings, and sculptures, in the art and life of those times.'

What was true for Germany was equally true for England, and for European Romanticism as such. In England, the line of medieval celebration is unbroken, though richly varied, from an early emphasis in Richard Hurd's *Letters upon Chivalry and Romance* (1762), which declared that [Edmund] Spenser's *Faerie Queene* had unity of design in the manner of a Gothic cathedral: 'When an architect examines a *Gothic* structure by *Grecian* rules, he finds nothing but deformity. But the *Gothic* architecture has its own rules, by which when it comes to be examined, it is seen to have its merit, as well as the Grecian.' The emerging Romantic rage for the medieval, as clearly represented in Hurd, eventuated in [Walter] Scott's *Ivanhoe* and *Marmion*, in Keats's *La Belle Dame sans Merci* and *Eve of St. Agnes*, and still later in [Alfred] Tennyson's *Lady of Shalott* and *Idylls of the King* and [William] Morris's *Haystack in the Floods* and *Defence of Guinevere*. Indeed, it is hardly possible to overestimate, however difficult it may be to comprehend the ramifications of, the importance of medieval imagining for Romanticism.

1. Referring to political thinker Jean Jacques Rousseau and poet George Gordon Byron

Scarcely less important, however, is the emphasis on visionary orientalism. [Samuel Taylor] Coleridge, who rendered rich homage to Romantic medievalism in his *Christabel*, rendered equally rich homage to Romantic orientalism in his *Kubla Khan*. Just as the all-pervading breath of the medieval is found not only in high Romanticism, but as the conditioning climate for the popularly orientated Gothic novels, and—still more intertwined in the popular bases of nineteenth-century culture—in the architecture of clapboard houses in the American Middle West, so too does Romantic orientalism appear in dispersed and divergent forms, ranging all the way from [Lord] Byron's having his portrait taken in oriental garb to [Arthur] Schopenhauer's using the philosophy of India as an element in his own philosophic nihilism. A standard secondary work on Emerson is called *Emerson and Asia*, and [Friedrich] Schlegel in 1808 produced an influential treatise called *Uber die Sprache and Weisheit der Indier*. Indeed, both Friedrich Schlegel and his brother Wilhelm actually learned Sanskrit, and Wilhelm translated the *Bhagavad-Gita* and the *Ramayana* into Latin.[2]

The philological labours of the Schlegel brothers were here harvesting a Sanskritist tradition inaugurated in the late eighteenth century by the Briton Sir William Jones, and sustained by their German contemporaries, the scholars Franz Bopp and Jakob Grimm. Alongside the imaginations of scholars, the imaginations of poets were also inflamed by oriental visions. Victor Hugo's poems, *Les Orientales* are no less significant of this fact than [Johann] Goethe's poems called *West-östlicher Divan*, Byron's *Turkish Tales* no less significant than [Thomas] Moore's *Lalla Rookh, an Oriental Romance*. [François] Chateaubriand, [Gérard de] Nerval, and [Alphonse] Lamartine, among others, all actually journeyed to the East and left records of their travels. In short, it may sometimes seem that 'It is in the Orient', as Friedrich Schlegel proclaimed in 1803, 'that we must seek the highest Romanticism.'

OTHER ROMANTIC MOTIFS

The world of dreams and the world of drugs offered alternative realms of escape. Indeed, both were intertwined with one another, as well as with the geographic and temporal

---

2. The *Bhagavad-Gita* is a Sanskrit poem that most Hindus regard as their most important text. The *Ramayana* is a Sanskrit epic about the life of the prince Rama.

otherness of medievalism and orientalism. Coleridge's *Kubla Khan*, cited above as witness to Romantic orientalism, is also witness to dreams and drugs, for its subtitle is 'A Vision in a Dream', and it is prefaced by a note explaining its inception in an opium dream. [Thomas] De Quincey, too, intertwined Romantic dreaming, Romantic drug-taking, and Romantic orientalism in his *Confessions of an English Opium-Eater:*

> Southern Asia, in general, is the seat of awful images and associations. . . . It contributes much to these feelings that Southern Asia is, and has been for thousands of years, the part of the earth most swarming with human life, the great *officina gentium.* Man is a weed in those regions. The vast empires, also, into which the enormous population of Asia has always been cast, give a further sublimity to the feelings associated with all Oriental names or images. In China, over and above what it has in common with the rest of Southern Asia, I am terrified by the modes of life, by the manners, and the barrier of utter abhorrence, and want of sympathy placed between us by feelings deeper than I can analyze. . . . All this, and much more than I can say or have time to say, the reader must enter into before he can comprehend the unimaginable horror which these dreams of Oriental imagery and mythological tortures impressed upon me.

Other emphases of Romanticism were a preoccupation with melancholy, and a preoccupation with solitude. 'J'écoute, j'appelle, je n'entends pas ma voix elle-même,' exclaimed Senancour's Oberman in 1804 . . . 'et je reste dans un vide intolérable, seul, perdu, incertain, pressé d'inquiétude et d'étonnement, au milieu des ombres errantes, dans l'espace impalpable et muet.'—I listen, I call, I cannot even hear my voice, and I am left in an intolerable emptiness, alone, lost, uncertain, borne down by inquietude and astonishment, amidst errant shadows, in intangible and silent space.' The Romantics exhibited a preoccupation with suicide as well. We need only cast our minds back to the suicides of [Goethe's] Werther, of Chateaubriand's Atala, of [Heinrich] Kleist's Penthesilea, of [Alfred Victor] Vigny's Chatterton, or to the declaration in Friedrich Schlegel's *Lucinde* that 'For a human being who is a human being, there is no death other than his own self-induced death, his suicide.'

Still other Romantic motifs cluster around the notion of process. The Romantic period was a world of accelerating change; governing philosophical ideas of immutable substance, as Ernst Cassirer has emphasized, had given way to protean ideas of function. Everything was in flux. The spectre that the *Communist Manifesto* in 1848 proclaimed to be haunting Europe, though designated as Communism, was more deeply the change from conceptions of substance to conceptions of process. As [Friedrich] Engels said later: 'The great basic thought that the world is not to be comprehended as a complex of ready-made *things*, but as a complex of *processes*, in which the things apparently stable, no less than their mind-images in our heads, the concepts, go through an uninterrupted change of coming-into-being and passing-away . . . this great fundamental thought has . . . thoroughly permeated ordinary consciousness.'

Everything was in flux. The very nature of poetry was conceived as flux, and rigidities of form and genre were washed away in the current.

The Importance of Imagination

James Engell

In the following article, James Engell explains why the concept of imagination is central to Romanticism. Although imagination is an element of all fiction, to the Romantics it was a force that could unite man with nature and matter with spirit. The Romantics used imagination in contrast to the sterile and mechanistic beliefs that pervaded the eighteenth century, most notably neoclassic formalism and materialism. However, the Romantics did not reject the thinking of all their predecessors; according to Engell, imagination serves as a link between the Enlightenment and Romanticism. Engell is a consulting editor for the *Journal of the History of Ideas* and a professor of English and comparative literature at Harvard University.

Though the concept of the imagination is the quintessence of Romanticism, that brilliant phase in art and thought did not itself create the idea of imagination. The reverse happened. Far more than any other one thing, this idea shaped and sustained Romanticism, which itself might be described as the mingled achievements of a number of individuals who in their own characteristic ways, shared a faith in imaginative power. Romanticism grew around the imagination in the manner that a storm masses around a vortex, a central area that differs in pressure from the surrounding space. If that area vanishes—if the idea is taken away—there will be only light and aimless winds. The attracting and unifying force of the imagination made Romanticism in the first place. Without that force the period would have become something radically different, its poetry and thought fragmented and disappointing.

Excerpted from James Engell, *The Creative Imagination: Enlightenment to Romanticism.* Copyright © 1981 The Presidents and Fellows of Harvard College. Reprinted with permission from Harvard University Press, Cambridge, MA.

A REACTION TO EARLIER TIMES

The idea of imagination, and with it Romanticism, was not only an outgrowth of the eighteenth century but a reaction to other tendencies and ideas in the century as well. This reaction was hardly directed at the open and inquiring spirit of the Enlightenment, and usually not at the last three or four decades of the century. [Samuel Taylor] Coleridge loved [Mark] Akenside and would hardly revolt against or condemn men like Francis Hutcheson, Hugh Blair, or Archibald Alison.[1] William Hazlitt thought [Thomas] Hobbes a great philosopher, and Hazlitt's second book was an abridgment of Abraham Tucker's *Light of Nature Pursued* (1768–1777). [William] Wordsworth read widely in eighteenth-century aesthetics, psychology, and moral philosophy. [John] Keats dedicated *Endymion* to the memory of Chatterton. The German Romantics often took issue with [Immanuel] Kant but rarely, if ever, regarded him as a sworn enemy. [Anthony Ashley Cooper] Shaftesbury, [Benedict] Spinoza, and [Gottfried] Leibniz were "discovered," debated, and revered.

The Romantics were not denouncing the whole eighteenth century; they wanted to repudiate certain aspects of thought and literary practice, especially those associated with neoclassic formalism, materialistic theories of mind and body, and atomistic philosophy. The bugbears of the Romantics, figures against whom the concept of the imagination was used as a weapon, hardly included Adam Smith with his belief in sympathy, William Duff on original genius, or [Johannes] Tetens on the qualities of poetic power. Rather the reaction was against the narrowly sterile and mechanistic side of previous generations. The Germans were especially concerned with casting off France's cultural imperialism. But more than an indictment of particular men, Romanticism was a reaction against a popular and social condition, an intellectual atmosphere in which large numbers of second and third-rate minds held power. In simplifying [John] Locke, popularizers had made him more rigidly mechanistic. The reaction to [Alexander] Pope was real enough. But although it was directed at him in name, much of the underlying cause was that the very kind of scribblers satirized and ab-

1. The three men were key eighteenth-century thinkers. Hutcheson was a philosopher; Blair was a preacher and literary critic; and Alison was a philosopher and the author of "Essays on Nature and the Principles of Taste."

horred by Pope and [Jonathan] Swift had, by 1760, become no less common. They walked the streets in flesh and blood. They clogged Grub Street. They got poetry and books published. [Samuel] Johnson, who virtually dismissed the unities of time and place on the basis of the audience's capacity for imaginative response, lampooned mechanical critics and thinkers in his series on Dick Minim in the *Idler* (Nos. 60–61). Yet thirty to fifty years later, the tendency in reacting to a popular ethos and in attacking a vested interest of thought and a literary establishment that seemed crusty was to select figures like Pope, Johnson, and Locke. They became symbols—often erroneously—of a pervading and undistinguished mass of ideas and conventions that were more formal and mechanistic than any they had ever believed in themselves. The Colley Cibbers and Thomas Rymers and Soame Jenynses[2] were not scathed in the Romantic period because they had already been reduced to size by the Johnsons, Popes, and Swifts.

The leading writers and minds of the late eighteenth and early nineteenth century recognized this fact most of the time. They knew that the history of letters and thought is diverse. There is not one important thinker on the imagination who did not owe a debt to several writers in the period from 1660 to 1760. When the Romantics leapt back to a love of the Elizabethan, or of [Greek philosopher and rhetorician] Longinus, or of the imagination found in Homer and Shakespeare, they continued a trend in taste fostered for a century before them.

Reaction, then, was part of the growth of the idea of imagination, but in a special way. The reaction was, in substance if not in polemics, more a case of the later decades of the eighteenth century overturning an abstract and mechanistic formalism found in the first half of the century, than a case of Romanticism throwing off the weight of the previous hundred years as a whole.

A Bridge Between Man and Nature

The idea of the imagination forms a hinge connecting the Enlightenment and Romanticism. It pivots and swings from one period to the other in a fashion that tells more about both of them than does any other point of contact. In a larger

2. Cibber was an English actor and dramatist who served as England's poet laureate from 1730–57. Rymer was an English historian of the seventeenth and eighteenth centuries. Jenyns was a poet and a member of parliament in the mid–eighteenth century.

perspective, the medieval and Renaissance world-views end and the classical tradition in literature wanes as the idea of the imagination becomes dominant. It introduces the modern era. During the century and a half from 1660 to 1810, the Great Chain of Being[3] enjoyed its last viable influence. The concept of imagination replaced it. The two ideas are not antithetical; they have some common ground, especially in their more Platonic interpretations. Shaftesbury, Leibniz, [Joseph] Addison,[Mark] Akenside,[Friedrich] Schelling, and Coleridge all combine the two ideas. But the Great Chain of Being could no longer take the full brunt of philosophical inquiry, nor support a view of man and nature, or of God, that squared with empiricism, psychology, and the new sciences of chemistry, astronomy, geology, and biology. The imagination offers the dynamic and active. It is a force, an energy, not a state of being. It more easily explains the interchange of state and the transforming, organic qualities of psyche and nature. The imagination better solved the problem why God would create the boundless diversity of nature if He were self-sufficient unto Himself. In the Western tradition the idea of imagination, developed in the Enlightenment and triumphant in Romanticism, marks the end of an epoch stretching back 2500 years and introduces a new stage of thought and letters, now two hundred years in progress.

One reason for this key place in what Coleridge calls the history of the collective human mind is that so many gifted individuals saw in the imagination a power that could bridge the gulf between man and nature and knit the two together again. Since the seventeenth century when the new philosophy called "all in doubt," a haunting and almost sinister dualism had thrust its way into prominence. This split, a bifurcation of man and nature, upset the pattern of Western thought and overturned one of its most cherished goals of unity. The popular optimism associated with[Isaac] Newton's work and with the new science and its methods of proof could not heal this split. A mechanistic outlook simply strengthened the barrier between man and nature. Reason was popularly viewed less as an intuitional power with direct apprehension of nature and truth, and more as a

3. The Great Chain of Being is an idea that originated with the Greek philosopher Aristotle. According to Aristotle, the universe is in the form of a hierarchy, which starts at the top with God, the most perfect being, and works its way down, with humans midway down the ladder.

method of deduction. Mystical and Platonic writers, on the other side, were drawn onto a tactically dangerous terrain. They were being forced to prove, empirically, that the empiricists and mechanists were wrong.

The world and the cosmos seemed to operate according to principles that were either alien to or beyond common understanding. The principles could be learned only as the senses received them piecemeal from the external world or as the mind intuited them from an internal sensibility and store of innate ideas. The imagination held out hope and promised a reconciliation of this dualism. It could overcome the alienation between man and nature by establishing a power of knowledge and creation common to nature and the mind, a power Coleridge might call "connatural."

Samuel Taylor Coleridge

By the mid 1700s a rapid movement was under way to show that the idea of imagination, with one foot in the empirical and one foot in the ideal or transcendental, could bestride those two peninsulas of thought and, like a colossus, protect and unify the harbor between. The imagination could, in its dialectic, synthesize soul and body; it could unite man's spirit and affections with the concrete reality of nature. The imagination would solve the dilemma of dualism. Each thinker who treated the idea of the imagination with any perspicacity soon realized that this grand synthesis promised fulfillment in the art of creative genius.

IMAGINATION AND THE POWER OF ART

But the creative imagination was not a new system of thought, though several systems were built on it. Since it was a moving force, creative and active itself, it could express in art the aesthetic play or balance, and the final unity, between ideal and real, sensuous and transcendental, subjective and objective, the magic by which we perceive and create, and even the miracle by which the cosmos first took and is continuing to take shape. As an idea, it invigorated several "systems" and tended to erode the barriers separating them.

The creative imagination therefore promised to the arts a crowning role in philosophical thought, in knowledge, power, and even in religion. It could lead to grace and salvation. It could recapture the ideal of unity. Literature and art were elevated to a height and popularity they had never before enjoyed and from which they have yet to descend. The increasing confidence in the creative imagination from about 1740 on led poets and critics to trust and to believe in it, to sense that they had a mission not only to fabricate a new worldview, a reappraisal of man and nature, but even more to swaddle this thought and energy around human feelings in the forms, colors, and sounds of a rediscovered natural world.

The creative imagination became the way to unify man's psyche and, by extension, to reunify man with nature, to return by the paths of self-consciousness to a state of higher nature, a state of the sublime where senses, mind, and spirit elevate the world around them even as they elevate themselves. The new concept of the imagination enlarged the humanities and increased the expectations placed on secular art, and the promise and burden of those expectations continue today.

As the "high Romantics" receive and develop the concept of the imagination, it becomes the resolving and unifying force of all antitheses and contradictions. It reconciles and identifies man with nature, the subjective with the objective, the internal mind with the external world, time with eternity, matter with spirit, the finite with the infinite, the conscious with the unconscious, and self-consciousness with the absence of self-consciousness. It relates the static to the dynamic, passive to active, ideal to real, and universal to particular. The Homeric catalogue of polar opposites that make up man and the universe becomes a list of unities. Imagination becomes the process to understand and to view both the world and the self. The imaginative poet obtains a power that is the essence of inspiration (the Greek *enthousiasmos*). He is the voice of knowledge, wisdom, and beauty, the creator of a metaphorical language that identifies one thing or spirit with another and expresses man's harmony with nature.

Late eighteenth-century and romantic writers used the figure of Proteus[4] to invoke the power of imagination, to per-

---

4. Proteus is a Greek mythological figure, the shepherd of the deep, who could change himself into any shape.

sonify what was called its "lively" force, and sometimes to give it a religious and Hellenic flavor. Coleridge and August Schlegel refer to Shakespeare as a Proteus, as does Hazlitt, but as early as 1774 William Richardson describes Shakespeare as "the Proteus of the drama; he changes himself into every character, and enters easily into every condition of human nature." To modify imagination with the word "protean" may seem a tautology. But the use suggests at least three important ways to look at the complex story we face. First, the imagination was an idea that operated through and changed numerous areas of thought. It generated other ideas. It touched the arts and literature profoundly, and with them philosophy. Aesthetics, morality, and religion shared it, though it was never interpreted in quite the same way. In poetry the imagination became responsible for overall poetic "genius" and for the gift of particular and striking characterizations. It could organize a composition, whether lyric, epic, or dramatic, into a whole whose patterns emerge from an internal *Geist* and not from an externally predetermined form.

Second, although an idea may have a life of its own, ideas that remain aloof from fresh and individual treatment are, as Alfred North Whitehead said, inert. They become moribund and die. After everyone agrees about an idea for a long enough period of time, they kill it. The imagination luckily never acquired a monolithic profile. As it is touched and used by each individual, it obtains a separate life, and all the interacting, inheriting, disowning, and reconciling of these separate lives form the idea at large, which is what we see on the gross canvas of history and literature. The story of an idea is a story about people, many related stories of many men and women. What Keats thought about the imagination differs, though not utterly, from Hobbes's view. Blake and Locke were not yoked together by W.S. Landor in his *Imaginary Conversations.* Perhaps Landor lacked the imagination for it. But the distance between those men is not one of years and natural conviction alone. It is also a distance created by the thoughts of other men who are intermediaries direct and indirect. The progress of the imagination is like a long play. It is dramatic over decades and will get nowhere unless the characters are different, and unless they themselves change with the news and action brought by others who exit early or enter late. The imagination is also protean, then, in the diverse and personal identities of individual agents who are its real life.

Last, as we enter the culmination of the Enlightenment from 1740 to 1760 and then pass into Romanticism, we discover a haunting and wonderful phenomenon. Many of the individuals who fall in love with the concept of the imagination—Coleridge, Blake, Schelling, Shelley, Tetens—have such capacious identities of their own, or at least offer such new and expansive views of the world, that each one of them is transformed and elevated. They are men of force and energy. They exemplify, as Shakespeare exemplified to them, that imagination can free us from a self-centered world. Each mind, as it exercises and acts out its particular faith in the imaginative power, becomes protean. Just as individuals change the nature of the idea by their own interpretation and use, so the idea changes the individual. The imaginative poet or thinker seems to feel and know, from the inside, the experience of other lives. And he touches us because he is touched by humanity.

Nature as Inspiration

Heather Coombs

In the following viewpoint, Heather Coombs explains
how nature inspired the Romantics. To the Romantic
writers, the natural world provided a new set of spiritual values. Mountains, for example, embodied the
best elements of nature—besides being beautiful,
they were a source of moral inspiration and intense
feelings. The Romantics, particularly William Wordsworth, John Keats, and Percy Bysshe Shelley, also
sought to enter into harmony with nature. They believed a better society would come if people rejected
materialism and returned to the pure emotional state
found in being one with nature. Poems that typify
this view include Wordsworth's "The Prelude" and
Shelley's "The Cloud." Coombs is the author of *The
Age of Keats and Shelley*, the book from which this
viewpoint was excerpted.

To the Romantic poets, to Wordsworth at the end of the eighteenth century, as to Keats and Shelley, twenty years later,
the natural world was not simply pretty; nor was it attractive
because it offered an *escape* from reality. On the contrary, its
importance lay in its ability to offer a completely new set of
spiritual values.

The first move towards this view of nature came with the
realization that order, neatness and control, in nature as in
man, do not necessarily make for greatness and nobility.
The German poet [Johanne] Goethe—in his novel *Sorrows
of Young Werther*, published in 1774, and extremely influential in England—expresses this theme through the mouth of
the young painter:

> Nature alone is infinitely rich, and Nature alone forms the great
> artist. Much can be adduced in favour of rules . . . The man
> who models himself on them will never produce anything infe-
> rior or in bad taste . . . but there will be an end to . . . his art.

Keats was later to express precisely the same views when he

wrote to his publisher that *'if Poetry comes not as naturally as the Leaves to a tree it had better not come at all'.*

THE MEANINGS OF MOUNTAINS

An early manifestation of the growing taste for wildness and the obviously uncontrolled was the new fashion for mountain scenery. It may seem surprising today, when mountaineering is a popular pastime and Alpine views have become a cliché, that, until the late eighteenth century, mountains were generally considered simply a nuisance. . . .

And yet [in 1739] the poet [Thomas] Gray wrote to his mother from Turin, where he was travelling with Horace Walpole, describing the experience of crossing the Alps in glowing terms:

> *The immensity of the precipices, the soaring of the river and torrents that run into it, the huge crags covered with ice and snow, and the clouds below you and about you are objects it is impossible to conceive without seeing them.*

To his friend Richard West, he was even more expansive:

> *I do not remember to have gone ten paces without an exclamation, that there was no restraining: Not a precipice, not a torrent, not a cliff, but is pregnant with religion and poetry.*

As this idea that mountains embodied all the most wonderful qualities of nature grew more popular, they became part of the taste for 'the sublime'. This was a term applied to anything beyond control and comprehension which yet aroused feelings of wonder and awe. A good description of what the eighteenth-century writer meant by the sublime can be found in the essay 'On the Sublime and Beautiful' by the statesman Edmund Burke, published in 1756. He describes how 'the sublime' must arouse deep feelings, more of terror than delight:

> *Whatever is fitted in any sort to excite the ideas of pain and danger, that is to say, whatever is in any sort terrible, or is conversant about terrible objects, is a source of the sublime; that is, it is productive of the strongest emotion which the mind is capable of feeling.*

Such ideas were strengthened and popularized by the mountainous scenery included in best-selling works of fiction, such as Mrs. [Anne] Radcliffe's *The Mysteries of Udolpho*, published in 1794, where the Alps are not only described, but specifically shown to arouse intense feelings. . . .

It is noteworthy that the mountains are not simply regarded as beautiful or breathtaking; their role is more positive and moral, for they arouse '*a finer spirit*'. And this is typical of the late eighteenth-century feeling for mountains which were seen as able to inspire the purity and realization of a better life such as [Jean-Jacques] Rousseau had felt could be found in a return to nature. Indeed, they themselves symbolized a return to nature, for mountains such as the Alps, or, nearer home, the Scottish Highlands, were inevitably the home of isolated communities unspoilt by much contact with a sophisticated, materialistic society. Both aspects of mountain life—the moral inspiration, and the return to simplicity—can be seen in the poetry of William Wordsworth, which emerged upon the English literary scene at the end of the eighteenth century, and which was both a result and a cause of a popular desire to 'return to nature'.

WORDSWORTH'S VIEWS ON NATURE

Wordsworth was one of the 'Lake' school of poets, that is, a group of three poets (himself, Coleridge and Southey) who lived in the English Lake District. Wordsworth, in particular, advocated a return to simple language and homely events in poetry. He decided to '*choose incidents and situations from common life*' and many of the '*incidents*' he described show the moral effects of nature—especially the hills and mountains of the north of England—upon himself and on simple country folk. In his autobiographical poem *The Prelude*, subtitled '*Growth of a Poet's mind*', he describes how his love of nature and, at the same time, his fear of its awesomeness— its sublimity—moulded and formed him. His was, after a fashion, an *Emile*[1] type of education where the child learns by experience and by the impressions borne in upon him from the natural world, whether these impressions be peaceful or disturbing:

> *Dust as we are, the immortal Spirit grows*
> *Like harmony in music; there is a dark*
> *Inscrutable workmanship that reconciles*
> *Discordant elements, makes them cling together*
> *In one society. How strange that all*
> *The terrors, pains and early miseries,*
> *Regrets, vexations, lassitudes interfused*
> *Within my mind, should e'er have borne a part,*
> *And that a needful part, in making up*
> *The calm existence that is mine when I*
> *Am worthy of myself! Praise to the end!*

1. A novel by Jean-Jacques Rousseau

Thanks to the means which Nature deigned to employ;
Whether her fearless visitings, or those
That came with soft alarm, like hurtless light
Opening the peaceful clouds; or she may use
Severer interventions, ministry
More palpable, as best might suit her aim.

Inspired partly by the growing taste for Wordsworth's poetry, after initial harsh critical reaction, and partly by the continuing interest in the exotic and the wild, tourists flocked to the Lake District, which suddenly became an amazingly popular tourist resort. Simultaneously, the fashionable liking for mountains was being reflected in the work of artists such as Richard Wilson, whose painting *Cader Idris* depicts the angular sharpness of his native Welsh scenery. Early pictures by [J.M.W.] Turner, such as *Buttermere Lake,* and such paintings as *Valley of Zion* by John Cozens, all celebrated the growing interest in the inspirational quality of mountainous scenery—an interest which received a new impetus from the novels of Walter Scott. As Scott's popularity grew—and it grew at an incredible rate, so that his novels were sold by the thousands on the day of publication—the mountains of Scotland became familiar in imagination to countless men and women who never had, and never would, actually see them. In Scott, as in Mrs. Radcliffe and Wordsworth, mountains are not merely breathtaking to look at, though they are certainly that; they ennoble the feelings and inspire the soul. . . .

Exactly the same idea is apparent in . . . Mary Shelley's *Frankenstein,* published in 1818, a year after Scott's tale of the wild outlaw achieved such popularity. Frankenstein, the scientist, stricken with grief at the outcome of his creation of a monster, roams the Alps in an attempt to calm his mind. He describes the *'abrupt sides of vast mountains'* where the only sounds are those of the avalanche or cracking ice. Far from being made gloomier by his surroundings,

These sublime and magnificent scenes afforded me the greatest consolation that I was capable of receiving. They elevated me from all littleness of feeling, and although they did not remove my grief, they subdued and tranquilised it.

NATURE INSPIRED THE ROMANTIC POETS

By the time Keats and Shelley were writing, then, the view of Nature as a well-ordered machine in which man was a necessary cog had given place to a view of Nature as the great inspirer, the purifier of souls, the healer of men as opposed to the corrupt influence of society. Nature, one might say, was now on the side of the revolutionary elements in the state, and it was no accident that the months of the new French Revolutionary Calendar were named, not after great

NATURE: A MULTIFACETED WORD

Stephen Prickett, a professor of English literature at the University of Glasgow in Scotland, explains how "nature," a key word in Romanticism, can be defined many different ways.

[Nature] is a key word, yet it is a word of such blanket meaning that all attempts at definition seem to founder at the onset. It can, for instance, mean any one of the following:

1. The 'cosmos': the sum total of everything is clearly 'nature' in its broadest sense, but in fact the word is more normally used as *a contrast* with something else. For example:
2. The 'world of sense-perception' (as distinct from the 'supernatural');
3. The 'country' (as distinct from the town);
4. 'What grows organically' (as distinct from an artifact that is made by man);
5. 'What happens spontaneously' (as distinct from what is 'unnatural', either because it is laboured as contrived, or, as in 'unnatural vices', because it is held to be denying, perverting or thwarting a quality or instinct believed to be innate). . . .

The last three notions—the 'rural', the 'organic' and the 'spontaneous'—are central to some aspects of Romanticism, and play a key part in the poetry of Wordsworth, for example. . . .

Yet 'nature' can also be thought of in a much more active and manipulative role, as in:

6. 'The life-force': This is a very ancient meaning indeed, going back to classical times and the Greek mystery cults. Two Latin tags bring out an ambiguity that has always haunted the word.
   (a) *Natura naturans*: literally 'nature naturing'. Nature is here experienced as an active, dynamic power in a constant process of change and renewal. It is in complete contrast with
   (b) *Natura naturata*: literally 'nature natured'. Here nature is frozen, is laid out on a slab for dissection and scientific investigation. The observer does not participate. It is against this view that Wordsworth was reacting in his famous line from *The Tables Turned:* 'We murder to dissect.'

Stephen Prickett, "Romantic Literature," from Stephen Prickett, ed., *The Romantics.* New York: Holmes & Meier, 1981.

leaders, but after the seasons and types of weather.

When John Keats set off with Charles Brown on a walking tour of the Lake District and the Scottish Highlands in
the summer of 1818, he was following the general trend; he
was not going for the exercise, nor just to see beautiful
views, but to be improved morally, elevated emotionally,
and inspired poetically:

> *I should not have consented to myself these four Months tramp-
> ing in the highlands but that I thought it would give me more
> experience, rub off more Prejudice, use (me) to more hardship,
> identify finer scenes, load me with grander Mountains, and
> strengthen more my reach in Poetry, than would stopping at
> home among Books even though I should reach Homer.*

He found some inspiration, certainly, but he also found a
great deal of discomfort and made the discovery that one can
have too much of a good thing. Writing to his friend Ben-
jamin Bailey in July, 1818, he complains:

> *I have been among wilds and Mountains too much to break
> out much about the(i)r Grandeur.*

This feeling seems to have stayed with him, for certainly
mountains do not figure largely in his poetry, unlike that of
Shelley—though admittedly Shelley had seen the Alps. For
Shelley mountains were extremely important symbolically,
and do represent a real source of inspiration and regeneration. This can be seen in *Prometheus Unbound*, for though
Prometheus is

> *Nailed to this wall of eagle-baffling mountain,*
> *Black, wintry, dead, unmeasured; without herb*
> *Insect, or beast, or shape or sound of life,*

his suffering on the mountain seems to endue him with the
qualities of the mountain, its strength and power—what Mary
Shelley in her notes on the poem calls *'fortitude and hope and
the spirit of triumph'*. Similarly, it is on a mountain-top that
Laon and Cythna in 'The Revolt of Islam' fulfil their love and
achieve the sense of calm fortitude which enables them to
face the tyrant:

> *Through the desert night me sped, while she alway*
> *Gazed on a mountain which we neared, whose crest*
> *Crowned with a marble ruin, in the ray*
> *Of the obscure stars gleamed . . . now*
> *A power, a thirst, a knowledge, which below*
> *All thoughts, like light beyond the atmosphere*
> *Clothing its clouds with grace doth ever flow*
> *Came on us, as we sate in silence there,*

Beneath the golden stars of the clear azure air.

Keats and Shelley may depict different aspects of nature, but they share a common purpose in attempting to show, as Wordsworth had, the unity of all creation. For Wordsworth, it is a mystical unity, when his very soul leaves his body and he becomes at one with nature:

> *even the motion of our human blood*
> *Almost suspended, we are laid asleep*
> *In body, and become a living soul:*
> *While with an eye made quiet by the power*
> *Of harmony, and the deep power of joy,*
> *We see into the life of things.* ["Tintern Abbey"]

For Shelley, most important is the Platonic sense of an ideal universe—a millennium, a new Hellas [Greece]—where perfect man will be at one with essential nature, for:

> *All things by a law divine*
> *In one spirit meet and mingle.* ["Love's Philosophy"]

And to Keats, there is the belief, repeated over and over in letters and poetry, that there is an essential harmony between all things, and that the poet must continually partake of the existence of all other creatures—

> *The Sun, the Moon, the Sea and Men and Women.*

SEEKING HARMONY WITH NATURE

But man's relationship with Nature is twofold; he is to be at one with her ultimately, but she herself is to be his teacher, and help him to attain that unity. As Wordsworth describes watching the flowers and being led to share their enjoyment, so that his heart *'dances with the daffodils'*, so Keats and Shelley both endeavour through a keen observation of nature to enter into the life of natural objects. In 'The Cloud', for example, Shelley *becomes* the cloud, singing in an insistent, rolling rhythm about the endless circular motion of his existence:

> *I am the daughter of Earth and Water*
> *   And the nursling of the sky*
> *I pass through the pores of the ocean and shores;*
> *   I change, but I cannot die.*
> *For after the rain when with never a stain*
> *   The pavilion of Heaven is bare,*
> *And the minds and sunbeams with their convex gleams*
> *   Build up the blue dome of air,*
> *I silently laugh at my own Cenotaph,*
> *   And out of the caverns of rain,*

> *Like a child from the womb, like a ghost from the tomb,*
> *I arise and unbuild it again.*

Keats, too, expresses the same sense of harmony with nature when he writes that *'if a sparrow come before my Window I take part in its existence and pick about the Gravel'*. So, in 'Ode to a Nightingale', he not only desires to *'fade away into the forest dim'*, but, through *'the viewless wings of Poesy'*, he partakes of the nightingale's existence and is *'Already with thee . . .'* On a different level, his ability to enter into another's existence is shared with his readers, when the apparently objective description of Lamia's change from snake to woman becomes of such intensity that we feel the agony ourselves—perhaps particularly because Keats jars our senses from complacency by the unnatural association of *'scarlet'* with *'pain'*. And Keats makes us further aware of the sense in which all experiences of man enter into a mystical harmony with nature by instinctively using imagery drawn from the natural world, even when describing man-made objects, like Madeline's window:

> *Innumerable of stains and splendid dyes*
> *As are the tiger-moth's deep-damask'd wings,*
>> ["The Eve of St. Agnes"]

or a human emotion, like melancholy—

> *when the melancholy fit shall fall*
> *Sudden from heaven like a weeping cloud*
> *That fosters the droop-headed flowers all*
> *And hides the green hill in an April shroud.*
>> ["Ode on Melancholy"]

Man at one with nature, then, is the desire of the Romantics. But it is not a sentimental rusticity which they desire, not the kind of temporary escape from sophistication which made eighteenth-century court ladies play at being milkmaids for an afternoon or which led to the Augustan vogue for pastoral poetry. For Keats and Shelley and their contemporaries, a return to the pure and unmaterialistic emotions associated with rural as opposed to urban life, and wild as opposed to cultivated scenery, was an essential precursor of the new kind of society which they felt to be so eminently desirable.

The Meditative Qualities of Romantic Poetry

M.H. Abrams

The Romantic lyrics—short poems that express personal emotion—evolved from earlier poetic forms, M.H. Abrams asserts. An important characteristic of the lyric was an emphasis on serious and sustained meditation. The meditation typically revolved around the poet's efforts to resolve an emotional crisis, in particular feelings of alienation and dejection, and this inner contemplation was often mimicked by the poet's meditation on a given natural landscape. Two earlier types of poems influenced the meditative qualities of the Romantic poems and their reliance on nature to mirror the inner turmoil of the poet. In the seventeenth century, George Herbert and other poets wrote metaphysical poems, which emphasized meditation on spiritual crises but described allegorical rather than specific landscapes. In contrast, so-called "local poems" offered personal reflections but were centered more on accurately describing specific locations and scenery instead of using nature as a foil. The Romantic lyrics borrowed elements from both predecessors by depicting serious meditations about specific locations that seemed to reflect the poet's mood. Abrams is a professor emeritus of English literature at Cornell University in Ithaca, New York as well as the general editor of the *Norton Anthology of English Literature*.

The greater Romantic lyric . . . as established by [Samuel Taylor] Coleridge, evolved from 'the descriptive-meditative

Excerpted from "Structure and Style in the Greater Romantic Lyric," from *The Correspondent Breeze: Essays on English Romanticism*, by M.H. Abrams, Foreword by Jack Stillinger. Copyright © 1984 M.H. Abrams and Jack Stillinger. Reprinted with permission from W.W. Norton & Company, Inc.

structure of the eighteenth-century local poem,[1] primarily
through the intermediate stage of [William Lisle] Bowles's sequence of sonnets. There remains, however, a wide disparity
between the Romantic lyric and its predecessors, a disparity
in the organization and nature of the meditation proper. In local poetry the order of the thoughts is the sequence in which
the natural objects are observed; the poet surveys a prospect,
or climbs a hill, or undertakes a tour, or follows the course of
a stream, and he introduces memories and ideas intermit-
tently, as the descriptive occasion offers. In Bowles's sonnets,
the meditation, while more continuous, is severely limited by
the straitness of the form, and consists mainly of the pensive
commonplaces of the typical late-century man of feeling. In
the fully developed Romantic lyric, on the other hand, the description is structurally subordinate to the meditation, and
the meditation is sustained, continuous, and highly serious.
Even when the initial impression is of the casual movement
of a relaxed mind, retrospect reveals the whole to have been
firmly organized around an emotional issue pressing for resolution. And in a number of the greatest lyrics—including
Coleridge's *Dejection*, [William] Wordsworth's *Intimations*,
[Percy Bysshe] Shelley's *Stanzas Written in Dejection* and *West
Wind*, [John] Keats's *Nightingale*—the issue is one of a recurrent state often called by the specialized term "dejection."
This is not the pleasing melancholy of the eighteenth-century
poet of sensibility, nor Bowles's muted self-pity, but a profound sadness, sometimes bordering on the anguish of terror
or despair, at the sense of loss, dereliction, isolation, or inner
death, which is presented as inherent in the conditions of the
speaker's existence.

THE INFLUENCE OF DEVOTIONAL POEMS

In the English literary tradition these Romantic meditations
had their closest analogue in the devotional poems of the
seventeenth century. In his study *The Poetry of Meditation*,
Louis Martz has emphasized the importance, for the religious poets we usually class as "metaphysical," of the numerous and immensely popular devotional handbooks
which undertook to discipline the casual flow of ordinary
consciousness by setting down a detailed regimen for evok-

1. Local poems are a type of poem common in the eighteenth century. The title named
a specific geographic location, while the poem described both the scene and the
thoughts that the scene suggested.

ing, sustaining, and ordering a process of meditation toward resolution. A standard sub-department was the "meditation on the creatures" (that is, on the created world) in order, as the title of Robert Bellarmine's influential treatise of 1615 put it, to achieve *The Ascent of the Mind to God by a Ladder of Things Created.* The recommended procedure, as this became stabilized at the turn of the century, tended to fall into three major divisions. The first involved what [Saint Ignatius of] Loyola called the "composition of place, seeing the spot"; that is, envisioning in vivid detail the person, object, or scene which initiates the meditation. The second, the meditation proper, was the analysis of the relevance to our salvation of this scene, interpreted analogically; it often included a turn inward to a close examination of conscience. The last specified the results of this meditation for our affections and will, and either included, or concluded with, a "colloquy"—usually a prayer, or discourse with God, although as Saint Francis de Sales advises, "while we are forming our affections and resolutions," we do well to address our colloquy also "to ourselves, to our own hearts . . . and even to insensible creatures."

Few seventeenth-century meditative poems accord exactly with the formulas of the Catholic or Anglican devotional manuals, but many of them unmistakably profited from that disciplining of fluid thought into an organized pattern which was a central enterprise in the spiritual life of the age. And those poetic meditations on the creatures which envision a natural scene or object, go on in sorrow, anguish, or dejection to explore the significance for the speaker of the spiritual signs built into the object by God, and end in reconciliation and the hope of rebirth, are closer to the best Romantic lyrics in meditative content, mood, and ordonnance than any poem by Bowles or his eighteenth-century predecessors. Good instances of the type are [Henry] Vaughan's *The Waterfall, Regeneration, Vanity of Spirit,* and "I walkt the other day (to spend my hour,) / Into a field"—an hour being a standard time set aside for formal meditation. *Regeneration,* for example, begins with a walk through a spring landscape which stands in sharp contrast to the sterile winter of the poet's spirit, finds its resolution in a sudden storm of wind which, as *spiritus,* is the material equivalent both of the breath of God and the spirit of man, and ends in a short colloquy which is a prayer for a spiritual dying-into-life:

> Here musing long, I heard
>   A rushing wind
> Which still increased, but whence it stirred
>   Nowhere I could not find. . . .
>
> Lord, then said I, on me one breath,
> And let me die before my death!

The two key figures of the outer and inner seasons and of the correspondent, regenerative wind later served as the radical metaphors in a number of Romantic poems, including Coleridge's *Dejection* and Shelley's *Ode to the West Wind.*

COLERIDGE AND HERBERT

Or consider the meditation on a creature which—at least in his later life—was Coleridge's favorite poem by one of his favorite lyrists, George Herbert's *The Flower.* Reflecting upon the annual death and rebirth of the plant, the poet draws a complex analogy with his own soul in its cycles of depression and joy, spiritual drouth and rain, death and springlike revival, alienation from God and reconcilement; in the concluding colloquy he also (as Coleridge and Shelley were to do) incorporates into the analogy the sterility and revival of his poetic powers:

> And now in age I bud again,
> After so many deaths I live and write:
>   I once more smell the dew and rain,
> And relish versing. O my only light,
>   It cannot be
>   That I am he
>   On whom thy tempests fell all night.

Herbert is describing the state of inner torpor through alienation from God known in theology as accidie, dejection, spiritual dryness, interior desolation; this condition was often analogized to circumstances of the seasons and weather, and was a matter of frequent consideration in the devotional manuals. As Saint Francis de Sales wrote, in his section "Of Spiritual Dryness and Sterility":

> Sometimes you will find yourself so deprived and destitute of all devout feelings of devotion that your soul will seem to be a fruitless, barren desert, in which there is no . . . water of grace to refresh her, on account of the dryness that seems to threaten her with a total and absolute desolation. . . . At the same time, to cast her into despair, the enemy mocks her by a thousand suggestions of despondency and says: "Ah! poor wretch, where is thy God? . . . Who can ever restore to thee the joy of His holy grace?"

Coleridge, during the several years just preceding *Dejection,* described in his letters a recurrent state of apathy and of the paralysis of imagination in terms which seem to echo such discussions of spiritual dryness: "My Imagination is tired, down, flat and powerless . . . as if the *organs* of Life had been dried up; as if only simple BEING remained, blind and stagnant!" "I have been . . . undergoing a process of intellectual *exsiccation* . . . . The Poet is dead in me ."

The Romantic meditations, then, though secular meditations, often turn on crises—alienation, dejection, the loss of a "celestial light" or "glory" in experiencing the created world—which are closely akin to the spiritual crises of the earlier religious poets. And at times Romantic lyrics become overtly theological in expression. Some of them include not only colloquies with a human auditor, real or imagined, and with what de Sales called "insensible creatures," but also with God or with a Spirit of Nature, in the mode of a formal prayer (*Reflections on Having Left a Place of Retirement, Ode to the West Wind*), or else of a terminal benediction. Thus Coleridge's *Frost at Midnight* falls into the ritual language of a blessing ("Therefore all seasons shall be sweet to thee")—a tactic which Wordsworth at once picked up in *Tintern Abbey* ("and this prayer I make. . . . Therefore let the moon / Shine on thee in thy solitary walk") and which Coleridge himself repeated in *Dejection* ("Visit her, gentle Sleep! with wings of healing. . . . To her may all things live, from pole to pole").

WHY ROMANTIC POETRY IS DIFFERENT

We must not drive the parallel too hard. There is little external evidence of the direct influence of the metaphysical poem upon the greater Romantic lyric; the similarity between them may well be the result of a common tradition of meditations on the creatures—a tradition which continued in the eighteenth century in so prodigiously popular a work as James Hervey's *Meditations and Contemplations* (1746–47). And there is a very conspicuous and significant difference between the Romantic lyric and the seventeenth-century meditation on created nature—a difference in the description which initiates and directs the process of mind. The "composition of place" was not a specific locality, nor did it need to be present to the eyes of the speaker, but was a typical scene or object, usually called up, as Saint Ignatius and other preceptors said, before "the eyes of the imagination" in order to set off and guide the thought by means of correspondences whose interpretation was firmly controlled by an inherited typology. The landscape set forth in Vaughan's *Regeneration,* for example, is not a particular geographical location, nor even a literal setting, but the allegorical landscape common to the genre of spiritual pilgrimages, from the *Divine Comedy* to *Pilgrim's Progress.* And Herbert's flower is not a specified plant, described by the poet with his eye on the object, but a generic one; it is simply the class of all perennials, in which God has inscribed the invariable signatures of His providential plan. In the Romantic poem, on the other hand, the speaker merely happens upon a natural scene which is present, particular, and almost always precisely located; and though Coleridge occasionally alludes to it still as "that eternal language, which thy God / Utters," the primary meanings educed from the scene are not governed by a public symbolism, but have been brought to it by the private mind which perceives it. But we know already that these attributes also had a seventeenth-century origin, in a poet who inherited the metaphysical tradition yet went on, as [John] Dryden and many of his successors commented, to alter it in such a way as to establish the typical meter, rhetoric, and formal devices of neoclassic poetry. The crucial event in the development of the most distinctive of the Romantic lyric forms occurred when John Denham climbed Cooper's Hill and undertook to describe, in balanced couplets, the landscape before his eyes, and to embellish the description with incidental reminiscence and meditation.

The Religious Views of the Romantic Poets

Hoxie Neale Fairchild

In the following article, Hoxie Neale Fairchild evaluates the Romantic poets' attitude toward religion and the effect of religion on their poetry. Fairchild argues that although religion improved Romantic poetry by giving the poets an important issue on which to focus, the work of many poets suffered because writing on such a vast topic was often difficult. Fairchild also notes that for the Romantics, religious feeling was often combined with pride. The Romantic poets were, as a whole, self-deifying, worshipping their genius and imagination. Fairchild was the author of books such as *The Noble Savage: A study in Romantic Naturalism* and a professor of English at Hunter College in New York City.

Romantic religion deserves much of the credit for the best qualities of romantic poetry. Deprived of their faith, these poets would have had nothing of large human significance to affirm or to deny. Possessing that faith, or struggling to possess it, they had a high hope and a deep sorrow, a style, a cause, a philosophy, and a cult. Obeying the urge toward infinite expansiveness, they "shot their being through earth, sea, and air,/Possessing all things with intensest love." To the great benefit of English poetry, they enriched the resources of imagery and rhythm, united man's feelings with external nature and with the glamorous past, revealed the beauty of neglected areas of life, gave a sweet and potent voice to the inmost depths of the human mind.

SHORTCOMINGS OF ROMANTIC POETS

And yet the religion of the romantics is equally responsible for the deficiencies of their art. The primary business of the poet is not to make a world, but to fashion works of art out of positive or negative responses to the qualities of a world which already exists. The romantic faith in imaginative power, however, can be satisfied only by the creation of a universe. The poems themselves are but confessedly inadequate blueprints of the cosmic mansion. For those who insist with [Robert] Browning that a man's reach should exceed his grasp the hugeness of the romantics' ambition establishes the greatness of their poetry, but others will object that all this straining to make poetry do the work of metaphysics and theology is damaging not only to religion but to art.

At their best these dreamers are also artists, masters of the technique of their instrument; but too often the joy of the craftsman is hampered by an excessively self-conscious awareness of the priesthood of genius. On the whole they think too much about being poets and not enough about writing poems. They are overly impressed by the powers and duties of the prophetic function. The urgency of their didactic obligation frequently impels them toward symbolism or even toward emotionalized rhetorical discussion. Artists are happier, and they give more happiness to mankind, when they take art a little less solemnly.

Neo-romantic scholars who describe these poets as great mystics unwittingly expose one of their most serious shortcomings. Since the religious implications of poetry are not mystical but sacramental, poetry and mysticism represent opposite poles of spiritual life. Admittedly the pinnacle of the romantic faith is a sense of cosmic interfusion. But so far as this experience is genuinely mystical it transcends the utmost powers of speech, while so far as it is laden with the sensuousness of genuine poetry it vitiates the mystical aspiration. Hence the feverish struggle to express the inexpressible through a mixture of concreteness and vagueness which stirs our emotions without completely satisfying the demands either of religion or of art.

There is a large tincture of traditional snobbery in the habit of regarding the lyric as an essentially inferior type. It is significant, however, that the longing for a vast spiritual synthesis does not enable these writers to build a long poem which is more than a loosely strung succession of short ones, while on the other hand it is much more encouraging to the expression of fleeting moods. Even the admirable lyrics, moreover, move us through the part rather than through the whole. Since the romantic faith is evanescent, uncertain, and fragmentary it prohibits the very ambition which it inspires. The cosmic model shifts her pose too bewilderingly to permit the artist to create a unity.

ROMANTIC SELF-ANNIHILATION

But in romantic art, of course, there is no model at all other than that provided by inward feeling. Since poetry of any type is basically subjective, these poets should not be reproached for being almost exclusively concerned with their personal emotions. It is fair to say, however, that if inwardness is to be fruitful for religion or philosophy or art it must achieve a harmonious relationship with a limiting outwardness, and that the romantic spirit denies this obligation. But just on the point of describing the subjectivity of the romantic poet as solipsistic, we remember the paradox which has plagued us. . . . Why does the romantic, at the very summit of his egotism, seem to desire the dissolution of his personal identity?

More than once I have tried to answer this question by saying that romantic self-annihilation, implying the removal of all boundaries and restrictions, represents the extremest form of romantic self-expansion. If my explanation is valid—and the poets themselves appear to accept it—the apparent anomaly becomes a clue to the whole problem of romantic belief. From the pragmatic point of view which this [viewpoint] has adopted, the only motive for a man's cultivation of any religion is his desire to obtain more peace, sureness, goodness, and strength than he now possesses by uniting himself with some extrapersonal being or cosmic force which has power to confer those qualities or from which they may be drawn. Even more strongly than most men the romantic poets are moved by this desire. But their genuinely religious aspirations are frustrated by their reluctance to believe in any force superior to the force of their own genius. The divine universal interfusion which they attempt to worship is merely the goal of their personal creativity. Nature, love, brotherhood, liberty, beauty—all the objects of their devotion—become so many ways of expressing the spiritual sufficiency and independence of man. And deified romantic man is the self-portrait of the poet, for what any individual asserts of humanity he asserts primarily of himself. My students are sometimes inclined to attach lofty spiritual significance to [Algernon] Swinburne's "Glory to man in the highest, for man is the master of things"; but when I invite them to delete "man" from this stirring line and substitute "Swinburne" or their own names, they laugh at the absurdity. With the exception of [Lord] Byron, the romanticists do not laugh. The failure of their attempt to glorify their egotism by means of reverential disguises brings them nothing but despair.

For the last time let us remind ourselves of what we have termed the "circularity" of the romantic religious experience. [Robert] Burns is a warm-hearted soul, but he uses the benevolism enjoined by his "religion of the bosom" as a means of obtaining membership in a select circle of exceptionally sensitive and enlightened spirits. Hence it becomes an expression of egotism rather than of brotherhood. As a lover of women he is even more obviously self-centered.

A SUMMARY OF RELIGIOUS VIEWS

[William] Blake, who seems at first glance the most ardently religious of the group, provides the most extreme example of self-deification. "Man can have no idea of anything greater than man. . . . All deities reside in the human breast. . . . Thine own humanity learn to adore." With the deepest reverence he worships a Jesus who is no more than a symbol of his own creative energy. God is man, man in Eternity is imagination, and imagination is the genius of William Blake.

[William] Wordsworth is set somewhat apart from his fellows by his more genuine objectivity and his desire for the security provided by extrapersonal law. It is all the more significant, therefore, that in the last analysis his interfusion-experience should prove to be the exploit of the "absolute power" of the imaginative will, a *fiat* of "the Godhead which is ours." When in revising *The Prelude* he substituted "man's power" for "my power" he made no essential change. Even after he had renounced

> That licentious craving of the mind
> To act the God amongst external things,

he hoped to derive from Christianity a sense of "Submission constituting strength and power." Even his warmest contemporary admirers granted that he was utterly self-willed. Had his reverence always been a subconscious means of obtaining a safe harbor within which his mind could sail about under the illusion of perfect liberty?

There is no need to retrace [Samuel Taylor] Coleridge's

"religion of I AM" through the mazes of his thought: it is obvious that from Ottery to Highgate he never contemplated anything but the ego which he simultaneously adored and loathed. Always he yearns to behold the ultimate reality as

> The whole one Self! Self that no alien knows!
> Self, far diffused as Fancy's wing can travel!
> Self, spreading still! Oblivious of its own,
> Yet all of all possessing!

A finished virtuoso of self-esteem, at the last he can transform even penitence into a source of pride.

The narcissistic quality of [Percy Bysshe] Shelley's aspiration was, I believe, sufficiently set forth in [another chapter from Fairchild's book]. With all his loving soul he sought a reflection of his self-centered goodness in nature, in society, in the heart of woman, and in the Spirit of the Universe. For him as for Blake his imagination is God, and a man precisely like himself is the only conceivable redeemer. In more discouraged moments he can draw almost equal satisfaction from admiration of his blameless sufferings.

In [Lord] Byron the arc of romantic religion is short-circuited by the very blatancy of his egotism. Because of his special psychological situation he both asserts and denies the impulse which dominates his fellows. He seeks inflation by means of liberalism, pantheism, and the cult of genius; but he is at once too lonely and too cynical to have any strong belief in these disguises of self-regard. He betrays romanticism in deriding his own bluster.

The romantic aspiration of [John] Keats is specialized but intense. Much more of an artist than the others, he tries to elevate sensuous beauty to the level of an object of devotion. But when he thinks of beauty he thinks of the great poets who create it; when he thinks of great poets he thinks of fame; and when he thinks of fame he thinks of his own baffled ambition.

Whatever a romantic poet appears to be devoted to, closer examination reveals that his worship curves backward upon himself. The same may be said of innumerable professors of other religions, but there remains a vast difference between remorsefully failing to surmount a human weakness and making a cult of that weakness. By nature Saint Paul is hardly less egotistic than Blake, but he does not identify his self-esteem with the law of the universe. In his worst moments he says, "I speak as a fool," not "I speak as a genius."

RELIGION AND HUMAN NATURE

Hence the beginning and the end of romantic religion is what old-fashioned folk call pride. All the loveliness that lies between results from the endeavor to impart some sort of numinous sanction to the craving for independent power. Thus romanticism originates in the deepest primordial sub-soil of human nature. Historically speaking, however, the so-called Romantic Movement represents the turning-point of a Titanic assertion of human self-sufficiency which had begun to manifest itself as a dominant movement of mind in the sixteenth century.

CHAPTER 2

The Romantic Poets

English
Romanticism

The Imagination of William Blake

Mark Richard Barna

According to Mark Richard Barna, William Blake's poetry and imagination rebelled against the cultural trends of his time. England in the eighteenth century was experiencing the Age of Reason and had become more interested in sciences and industry than in art or spiritual matters. Blake opposed the values of the Age of Reason, opting instead to write poetry that reflected his desire to create an earthly paradise, one in which divinity can be experienced in everyday life. Blake felt that such a paradise could be created because he believed that the creative power of humans was linked to the divine. Imagination was the key, because to Blake it was the realm in which people were in touch with divinity. Therefore, through art and poetry, people could experience the eternal while still existing in the temporal world. According to Barna, Blake's belief in the supremacy of imagination is seen most clearly in his poem "Jerusalem," and Barna uses that poem to illustrate his claims in the following essay. Barna is a freelance writer whose work has appeared in the magazines *World & I* and *Gnosis.*

O Come ye Nations! Come ye People! Come up to Jerusalem!

This was William Blake's message to his contemporaries. The problem was that few of them heard it, and even fewer understood it. Had he lived during the Italian Renaissance or in the age of Milton and Spenser (say, between 1560 and 1660), times when vision in art and poetry were appreciated, things might have been different.

THE AGE OF REASON

Blake was born in 1757, smack into the Age of Reason. England was preoccupied with the sciences and disillusioned with religious faith. The prophets were now Bacon, Newton, and Locke.

Francis Bacon (1561–1626) believed the Universe could be fully known by experiment. Isaac Newton (1642–1727) later demonstrated this by systematizing the Universe via rules and measures.

Extending Newton's principles into a general theory of knowledge, John Locke (1632–1704) argued in *An Essay Concerning Human Understanding* (1690) that the mind is limited to sensory perceptions and that divine inspiration is merely "the conceits of a warmed or overweening brain." "Reason," wrote Locke, "must be our last judge and guide in everything."

Joshua Reynolds, president of the Royal Academy, where Blake was a student, introduced Locke's theories into art. Discounting divine inspiration, Reynolds taught that great art copies nature and is directed by rules. "Mere enthusiasm will carry you but a little way."

Meanwhile, the Church of England had succumbed to the ideology of the age by winnowing out the ideals of the Protestant Reformation (inspiration, prophecy, and a God within) and lauding rational inquiry and moral codes. Blake called this Deism, "the worship of God in this world," and its morality "Self-righteousness, the selfish virtues of the Natural Heart."

Reason had replaced spirit. Through mythopoeic [mythmaking] poetry and symbolic art, Blake tried to change this.

THE VEIL OF VALA

Blake calls the world we see and experience in our normal, everyday manner Vala—a veil covering Eternity. Albion, who symbolizes England in Blake's myth, has fallen in love with Vala and can no longer imagine a life without her. "O I am nothing," he cries, "and to nothing must return again: / If thou withdraw my breath, Behold, I am oblivion." [from "Jerusalem"]

Vala's veil is "a Terror & a Curse!" because it conceals from Albion his true self; consequently, Albion feels alienated from and bored with his surroundings. Blake expresses this in the following passage from his epic poem "Jerusalem" (1804–1820): "The Sun is shrunk: the Heavens are shrunk / Away into the far remote: and the Trees & Mountains withered / Into indefinite cloudy shadows in darkness & separation." Human beings are experienced in similar fashion: "My sons exiled from my breast pass to & fro before me." [from "The Four Zoas"]

The sun, the trees, the mountains, and people no longer are divine to Albion; rather, the world seems empty of life and meaning, and Albion himself feels worthless, "a Worm seventy inches long." [from "Jerusalem"]

THE IMPACT OF THE FRENCH REVOLUTION

In Blake's age, nations were being transformed from agricultural to industrial societies, creating a huge neglected and increasingly angry industrial working class. When the French Revolution began in 1789, the British aristocracy, concerned that a similar revolution might occur in England, denied the working class the liberties of free press, free speech, and the rights of petition and assembly. Riots, attempts at organization, and frame breaking (an effort to end unemployment due to technology by vandalizing machines) steadily increased. The aristocracy, however, effectively, often viciously, maintained law and order. All the while the ruling and merchant classes became richer and the working class poorer.

Blake wasn't the only English poet disgusted by this. [William] Wordsworth and [Samuel Taylor] Coleridge were also incensed; and all three found hope in the initial success of the French Revolution. For them the revolution was not only a political and social crisis but an apocalypse, an augury of a coming earthly paradise.

The few successful years of the French Revolution parallel Blake's perfervid homage to unrestrained Energy. His heroic "giant form" in his poetry and art during this period is Orc, the revolutionary breaking the chains of oppression. He also wrote and engraved *The Marriage of Heaven and Hell* (1790–93), a book that glorifies human desire and mocks all restraint. "He who desires but acts not, breeds pestilence."

But history betrayed him; the revolution failed. A succession of disasters, beginning with the Reign of Terror,[1] compelled the poet to reassess his philosophy. (He would later repress publication of *The Marriage*.) Energy, he now saw,

---

1. Part of the French Revolution, the Reign of Terror was a war dictatorship that lasted from 1793–94 and was marked by an increase in executions, as more than 3,000 people were sent to the guillotine. It ended in July 1794.

was too easily perverted to oppressive and selfish ends. Like Wordsworth and Coleridge, Blake realized political revolution was no answer. In *America a Prophecy* (1793) he writes: "The stern Bard ceas'd, asham'd of his own song; enrag'd he swung / His harp aloft sounding, then dash'd its shining frame against / A ruin'd pillar in glittering fragments; silent he turned away."

And yet out of the despair came a new way of looking at life. The millennial hope for a heaven on earth by revolution was supplanted by the Romantic notion that heaven is in consciousness itself. Blake began to believe that England could apprehend an immediate earthly paradise by turning toward "the Poetic Genius," "the land of life," or, the term he favored, the Imagination.

THE POWER OF IMAGINATION

For most of us, *imagination* connotes something fanciful and nonexistent; for Blake it is the only reality. "Imagination is the real & eternal World of which this Vegetable Universe is but a faint shadow & in which we shall live in our Eternal or imaginative bodies, when these Vegetable Mortal bodies are no more." [from "Jerusalem"]

Remember, "worlds" for Blake are states of consciousness. When consciousness contracts, the everyday world appears. When perceptions open, consciousness expands to reveal a world usually experienced only in rare, exalted moments. Says Blake, "If Perceptive Organs vary, Objects of Perception seem to vary / If the Perceptive Organs close, their objects seem to close also." [from "Jerusalem"]

William Blake

Occasionally the poet takes this idea to its extreme, granting the eye of man unbridled authority to sculpt the world of matter: "Sometimes the Earth shall roll in the Abyss & sometimes / Stand in the Center & sometimes stretch flat in the Expanse, / According to the will of the lovely Daughters of Albion [England's working class]." [from "Jerusalem"]

Trusting his Imagination, Albion is once again united with Jerusalem, his eternal spirit. The effect is that the world, seemingly lifeless, is perceived by Albion as human—indeed as Albion himself. "Rivers, Mountains, Cities, and Villages / All are Human," says Blake in *Jerusalem*. And in the epic poem *The Four Zoas* (1805–1810) he writes:

> So man looks out at tree & herb & fish & bird & beast
> Collecting up the scattered portions of his immortal body
> . . . wherever a grass grows
> Or a leaf buds, The Eternal Man is heard, is seen, is felt.

For Blake, the world and universe is within "The Eternal Man," human consciousness. While in a state of vision, one realizes that nothing is separate from consciousness—that all is me seen afar. This is not a form of humanism, however, since the author of consciousness remains God. Indeed, Blake argued that both Man and God are co-Eternal; God did not create Man (as written in Genesis), because Man is as old as (and is) God.

Blake expresses this Gnostic/Hermeticist[2] doctrine when he says, "God is Man & exists in us & we in him," a statement provocatively similar to Jesus' assertion that "I am in the Father, and the Father is in me."

To perceive from the perspective of Vision, or the Imagination, as Blake usually called it, is to experience Eternity in everything, from the grandest starry expanse to particulars like sand and wild flowers.

> To see a World in a Grain of Sand
> And a Heaven in a Wild Flower
> Hold Infinity in the palm of your hand
> And Eternity in an hour [from "Auguries of Innocence"]

In Blake's late poetry, Orc is replaced by Los, the tireless artist working at his anvil forging the gospel of the Imagination. Obviously identifying with Los, Blake, in his preface to *Milton* (1804–1808), reveals his personal goal: to build on earth through imaginative art and poetry the heavenly paradigm, which is called Jerusalem in the Book of Revelation.

> I will not cease from Mental Fight,
> Nor shall my sword sleep in my hand,
> Till we have built Jerusalem,
> In England's green & pleasant Land.[3]

2. Gnostics are adherents to Gnosticism. Central to Gnosticism is the belief that the material world is evil because the true God did not create it. According to Gnostics, people can only be saved if they escape from the material world into the spiritual world. Hermeticism is attributed to Hermes Trismegistus and relates to Gnostic writings in the first three centuries A.D.　3. "Sword" refers to Blake's pens, paintbrushes, and engraving tools.

A RETURN TO REASON

William Blake's works became widely available in 1925, making him in a sense a poet/artist of the twentieth century. This is fitting, for his prophecy that societies would continue to secularize, causing an increase in materialism and scientism—and a correlative increase of feelings in people of worthlessness and alienation—have come to pass in our own century.

Many twentieth-century thinkers rely on reason to solve the mysteries of the human being. [Physiologist Ivan] Pavlov and [psychoanalyst B.F.] Skinner argued that human behavior is strictly mechanical, and Freud explained away all psychological states by reason alone. Carl Sagan's "fundamental premise about the brain is that its workings—what we sometimes call 'mind'—are a consequence of its anatomy and physiology and nothing more."

The Bible's pronouncement that "we are [God's] workmanship" no longer seems to ring true; for scientific studies and psychological experiments have reduced us to nerve fibers, blood, and predictable emotional responses—a worm seventy inches long. Such a view binds us to our narrowed perceptions, just as it bound (as Blake often pointed out) the inhabitants of Plato's cave, who thought their milieu was the only reality and never knew of the shining Light outside.

Responding to the ideology of the Age of Reason, Blake propounded pure idealism. "Mental things are alone Real; what is Call'd Corporeal Nobody Knows of its Dwelling Place." [from "A Vision of the Last Judgment"] Consciousness is true reality, asserts the poet, and is either our heaven or our hell. The seventeenth-century German theosophist Jacob Boehme, whom Blake acknowledged as a master, believed Creation is the imagination of God. A believer in the God within, Blake went further, asserting that the Imagination is the divine in man.

Blake was a visionary; he saw things (the angel Gabriel, the Virgin Mary, the ghost of a flea) "normal" people do not see, and he believed that what he saw was real rather than hallucinatory. This is what keeps him remote from us. So does his declaration that the earth shall roll in the abyss and stretch flat in the expanse, all at our will. But if we focus upon the cognitive implications of his philosophy, suddenly what seemed mad and exaggerated begins to make sense.

How glorious to direct our will toward seeing each person, each leaf and flower, each neon sign above a street, as holy, as me seen afar, and to know that the love and the thoughts of God reside perpetually within all of us. How glorious to see the sun, not as a fiery red disk, as we habitually do, but as "an Innumerable company of the Heavenly host crying Holy Holy Holy is the Lord God Almighty!" [from "A Vision of the Last Judgment"]

The Greatness of Wordsworth's "The Prelude"

Frank N. Magill

According to an essayist in *Masterpieces of World Literature,* "The Prelude" is not only one of the greatest poems of the romantic era but also William Wordsworth's most important work. While on one level "The Prelude" is an autobiographical work detailing key events in the poet's life and the growth of his poetic mind, it is also an epic poem that reflects upon key romantic tenets, such as the importance of nature and imagination. The transcendent quality is so strong in fact that ultimately the hero of the poem is not Wordsworth but the human imagination. *Masterpieces of World Literature* is an anthology that was edited by Frank N. Magill. Magill has edited numerous books on literature and history, including *Critical Survey of Poetry* and *English Literature—Romanticism to 1945.*

"The Prelude" is William Wordsworth's most important work; many critics regard it as the central poem of the English Romantic age. In this sustained autobiographical meditation in blank verse, Wordsworth adapts—in fact, revolutionizes—the conventions of the epic tradition to explore and dramatize the growth of his mind as a poet. A poem about imagination, memory, and selfhood, "The Prelude" addresses at the same time the interactions between the self and the forces outside it—Nature, mankind, and God. It is the vivid self-portrait of a great poet who came of age during a time of political, social, and intellectual revolution, and it delineates the dilemmas faced by a mind seeking truth as traditional values and systems of belief were called into question.

The poem exists in several versions, none of which was

called "The Prelude" by Wordsworth himself, who died leaving it untitled and unpublished. It was given its title by his widow, who published it in its final version in 1850, shortly after Wordsworth's death. Wordsworth viewed "The Prelude" as part of a projected philosophical poem, conceived as his magnum opus, called "The Recluse." Wordsworth never completed "The Recluse"; feeling that it was "a thing unprecedented in Literary history that a man should talk so much about himself," he was also reluctant to publish "The Prelude" by itself.

While he did not publish it, he painstakingly polished it. The 1850 text of "The Prelude" is based on a manuscript finished in 1839, itself the final result of three complete reworkings and a great number of small revisions of a poem begun in 1798. Of most interest to modern readers are the 1805 "Prelude" (thirteen books)—a complete draft of the poem which includes, in the fictionalized episode of Vaudracour and Julia, an account of Wordsworth's love affair in France during the French Revolution—and the 1850 "Prelude" (fourteen books), the version most frequently published. The 1850 "Prelude" differs from the 1805 text in several ways. Most important are its suppression of the Vaudracour and Julia episode and its many stylistic and tonal alterations. Wordsworth changed individual passages of verse to make them, in turn, smoother or clearer or more elaborate or—what is most interesting—more in keeping with Christian orthodoxy and less boldly personal. Readers seeking to witness the "growth of a poet's mind" (Mary Wordsworth's subtitle for "The Prelude") as fully as possible can best do so by studying the 1805 and 1850 versions comparatively. There are, in fact, a number of modern editions of "The Prelude" that print the texts of 1805 and 1850 on facing pages (references here will be to the 1850 version).

TURNING TO THE PAST

Wordsworth remarked in an 1805 letter that he began "The Prelude" "because I was unprepared to treat any more arduous subject, and diffident of my own powers." The first book of the poem dramatizes these feelings vividly. Although Wordsworth is self-consciously and preeminently a poet of memory, he departs from his usual practice at the opening to locate his concerns squarely in the present. Book 1 shows the poet in the process of discovering his own subject. It begins as Wordsworth, having escaped from the cares of the city, is contemplating his newfound freedom. "The earth is all before me," he exclaims, and goes on to celebrate the prospect of long months of leisure to enjoy himself and to write poetry. His celebration is short-lived, however, and he goes on to recount, in the past tense, how he soon felt thwarted, unable to compose a line. A time of self-examination ensued, during which Wordsworth found himself unable to choose a subject to write about, whether because of "some imperfection in the chosen theme" or because he felt inadequate to the task. His spirits droop; he feels "like a false steward who hath much received and renders nothing back."

At this point the poem takes a dramatic turn. Wordsworth reaches back to his early childhood, asking rhetorically whether Nature's fostering ministry to his growing soul was meant only to end in frustration. Clearly, it was not, for now his imagination becomes unblocked as he begins to muse upon childhood activities and to focus in detail upon a series of vivid memories—snaring woodcocks on a frosty night, plundering a raven's nest on a high, naked crag, stealing a boat in the moonlight and feeling admonished by the "unknown modes of being" that are a part of Nature. These and other recollections, fetching "invigorating thoughts from former years," help to steady the poet in his present distress, to revive his mind, and to move him toward the subject of the rest of "The Prelude." Whereas in the opening lines the earth was all before him, but he could not find a way to proceed, now at the closing of book 1, he knows where he is going—"The road lies plain before me"—and he is ready to address "a theme/ Single and of determined bounds": "the story of my life."

The process, dramatized in book 1, of turning to the past for aid in present difficulties is characteristically Wordsworthian, and later in the poem he will specifically articulate a theory of how "feeling comes in aid/ Of feeling, and diversity of strength/ Attends us, if but once we have been strong." This theory of the saving power of imaginative memory is one of Wordsworth's most famous ideas: There are in our existence spots of time, That with distinct pre-eminence retain A renovating virtue, whence, depressed By false opinion and contentious thought, or aught of heavier or more deadly weight, In trivial occupations, and the round Of ordinary intercourse, our minds Are nourished and invisibly repaired.

Such moments take place "from our first childhood," and are chiefly to be found Among those passages of life that give Profoundest knowledge to that point, and how, The mind is lord and master—outward sense The obedient servant of her will.

These lines are quintessentially Romantic in their assertion of the primacy of the human imagination. Not all of "The Prelude" is equally assertive or thoroughly selfconsistent, and much of its power and interest lie in Wordsworth's arguments with himself about the power of imagination as he formulates, discards, refines, and perfects hypotheses about it and about Nature. "The Prelude" is a poem of process and discovery, and of doubt as well as of assertion. Wordsworth's own life becomes a kind of test case on the subject of imagination, and many of "The Prelude's" highest moments turn upon it.

EDUCATION AND IMAGINATION

From book 2 on, spurred by the turn his mind took toward early childhood in book 1, Wordsworth follows a roughly chronological narrative of his life, interrupted at significant moments by recurrence to relevant "spots of time." Up through book 6, Wordsworth addresses the birth and early growth of his imaginative powers. Books 7 through 11 treat their impairment, and books 12 through 14 detail their eventual restoration.

Describing his school days in book 2, Wordsworth recounts at the same time his developing relationship with Nature as he makes the effort to put himself in touch with the sources of his identity. The effort is not without difficulty; musing on his boyhood, he often seems to himself "two consciousnesses, conscious of myself/ And of some other Being." Like many other Romantic poems, "The Prelude" is deeply concerned with epistemology, with the investigation of the origin, nature, methods, and limits of human knowledge.

The third book of "The Prelude" takes Wordsworth into his university days at Cambridge. There, in the face of his dislike of the formal curriculum and methods of instruction, he learned more and more to depend upon his own inner resources, aided by the remembered examples of the poets Geoffrey Chaucer, Edmund Spenser, and John Milton, and of great thinkers such as Sir Isaac Newton, "a mind for ever/ Voyaging through strange seas of Thought, alone."

Wordsworth's experiences at Cambridge point up one of his characteristic difficulties: He was uncomfortable in casual social situations and among large groups of people. Although a professed lover of mankind, he was essentially a solitary individual, and his most cherished human encounters were with other solitaries or with a few intimate friends and family members. In book 4, he celebrates his return home from Cambridge for summer vacation, reflecting that "when from our better selves we have too long/ Been parted by the hurrying world, . . ./ How gracious, how benign, is Solitude," especially when it has an "appropriate human centre." He illustrates this idea by describing a powerful encounter he had with a discharged soldier he met one

William Wordsworth wrote much of his poetry while living at Dove Cottage (pictured), located in England's Lake District.

evening on a road. Solitude also figures significantly in book 4, in Wordsworth's account of how one morning, witnessing a glorious sunrise, he experienced an epiphanic moment that left him with the conviction "that I should be, else sinning greatly,/ A dedicated Spirit." Most critics have viewed this episode as referring to Wordsworth's vocation as a poet.

Wordsworth moves even more deeply into his contemplation of the forces that shape human life and the desires that drive it in "The Prelude's" fifth book. Subtitled "Books," it recognizes the human longing for emotional and spiritual growth and immortality beneath all imaginative endeavors, particularly literary creation, mathematical thought, and the education of children. Wordsworth contemplates these endeavors in the contexts of human frailty and error and of the frightening and inevitable reality of death. He ponders human life as a terrible struggle to survive in spite of threats both from within and from without—educational systems that maim the human spirit, untimely illnesses and accidents that kill, natural catastrophes that bring widescale destruction. Wordsworth delineates this struggle most suggestively in book 5, in his description of a dream about an impending deluge that threatens to drown the entire world.

WORDSWORTH IN THE ALPS

Still, his faith in imagination holds steady. Indeed, Wordsworth's description in book 6 of a walking tour he took in the Alps shows how this faith was strengthened. Such tours were very popular in Wordsworth's day; in fact, they had become conventionalized. Tourists embarked in the anticipation of sublime emotional experiences at prescribed vistas and moments. Mont Blanc, for example, was not to be missed, and the very moment of crossing the Alps—of passing from an upward to a downward course—held the promise of great excitement. This very conventionalization of the sublime, however, depressed Wordsworth. He was "grieved" to find Mont Blanc "a soulless image on the eye." Climbing the road to the Simplon Pass, he and his companion lost their way, only to learn from a passerby native to the district that they had crossed the Alps unwittingly. At this point, Wordsworth breaks from his narrative of disappointment to an impassioned celebration of the creative power of the imagination. He recognizes that the human mind's power of expectation is infinitely greater than any earthly fulfillment could be, and that therefore the imagination is not tied to the earth: Our destiny, our being's heart and home, Is with infinitude, and only there; With hope it is, hope that can never die, Effort, and expectation, and desire, And something evermore about to be.

Wordsworth returns to his narrative to describe, in what has become one of the most celebrated passages of blank verse in the English language, how the landscape subsequently seemed transformed, in fact, apocalyptic in import: . . . The immeasurable height Of woods decaying, never to be decayed, The stationary blasts of waterfalls, And in the narrow rent at every turn Winds thwarting winds, bewildered and forlorn, The torrents shooting from the clear blue sky, The rocks that muttered close upon our ears, Black drizzling crags that spake by the way-side As if a voice were in them, the sick sight And giddy prospect of the raving stream, The unfettered clouds and region of the Heavens, Tumult and peace, the darkness and the light—Were all like workings of one mind, the features Of the same face, blossoms upon one tree; Characters of the great Apocalypse, The types and symbols of Eternity, Of first, and last, and midst, and without end.

The human mind and Nature, therefore, each in its own way, partake of and shadow forth the Divine and the eternal.

HOPE AND DESPAIR FOR HUMANKIND

From the Alps in book 6, Wordsworth descends in the seventh book into London, a "monstrous ant-hill on the plain/ Of a too busy world." His spirits sink, pulled down by his remembered impressions of the dehumanization of city life and the victimization there of women and children. The hideous realities of London impinge upon and threaten the imagination, which seems there to have scant place in and little hope for changing human society. Wordsworth leaves this confused, alienated, and alienating world of conflicting data, sense impressions, and moral problems to return in book 8 to the country, where the sources of his own identity lie. Book 8 provides a mental retrospect of the action of the whole poem thus far, and culminates in Wordsworth's assertion that his early love of Nature led him to the love of Man; its climactic image, appropriately, is one of man in Nature—a shepherd.

Wordsworth goes on in the next several books to recall his own hopes for humankind in general during the French Revolution. He shared these hopes with visionary thinkers like [philosopher and political theorist] Jean Jacques Rousseau, who asserted the natural goodness of human nature. The initial events of the Revolution were heartening to Wordsworth and seemed to him to be in the natural course of things. When England went to war with France, however, and with the shock of the Reign of Terror[1] and of France's new role as an aggressor against other nations, Wordsworth's expectations were shattered, his faith in humankind shaken. Having witnessed a split between the ideal and the real, between theory and fact, in the events in France, a comparable splitting occurred in his own soul. First his thoughts became divorced from his feelings, and, tyrannized by his abstract intellect's exhausting demand for formal proof of "all precepts, judgements, maxims, creeds," he "yielded up moral questions in despair." Next, he found himself out of touch with the physical world, as his "bodily eye" began to tyrannize over his imagination; he became overly concerned with the visual surfaces of the natural world and no longer experienced its moral, emotional, and spiritual power.

From book 12 on, Wordsworth narrates how his impaired imagination was restored, principally through the agency and examples of his beloved sister Dorothy and his wife Mary, and through his own remembrances of "spots of time" in his early life. His joyous account of this restoration leads him to conclude "The Prelude" triumphantly, with an apocalyptic vision he experienced ascending Mount Snowdon, a vision in which Nature became "the type/ Of a majestic intellect," the emblem of the human creative imagination, which is itself godlike. He assumes the role of prophetic poet, who will teach others of the beauty, power, and divine fabric of the mind of man.

"The Prelude" is epic in scope and victorious in outcome. Its battles, however, are not external but internal, as are its depths and heights. Its hero is not to be defined narrowly, as William Wordsworth, but broadly, as the human imagination.

---

1. Part of the French Revolution, it was a war dictatorship that lasted 1793–94 and was marked by an increase in executions, as more than three thousand people were sent to the guillotine. The Reign of Terror ended in July 1794.

Coleridge's "Rime of the Ancient Mariner" Is a Superior Romantic Ballad

John Spencer Hill

John Spencer Hill explains how in the poem "Rime of the Ancient Mariner," Samuel Taylor Coleridge takes the genre of Romantic ballads to a higher level than his predecessors. Coleridge's work uses the meters and rhyme schemes similar to earlier works by Bishop Thomas Percy and the supernatural elements of early ballads. According to Hill, however, "Rime of the Ancient Mariner" is superior to its predecessors because of the way Coleridge uses language and the common elements of ballads, such as repetition and internal rhymes, to depict the movement of the ocean and the ship as well as the emotional changes that take place within the Mariner. Coleridge's innovation can also be seen in the manner in which he uses age-old devices—such as invoking the supernatural—to serve the overall theme of his ballad. Previously such devices were merely decorative or shocking, but Coleridge employs them to reflect the inner turmoil of his title character. Prior to his death in 1998, Hill had taught English at the University of Ottawa and written and edited books on romantic poetry, including *A Coleridge Companion: An Introduction to the Major Poems* and the *Biographia Literaria*, from which this selection is excerpted.

Although it has occasionally been suggested that 'The Ancient Mariner' may profitably be read as a miniature epic or even a dramatic monologue, there is no doubt that Coleridge's poem is, first and foremost, a ballad. It is, as W.P. Ker

Excerpted from John Spencer Hill, *A Coleridge Companion: An Introduction to the Major Poems and the* Biographia Literaria. Copyright © 1983 John Spencer Hill. Reprinted with permission from Macmillan Press Ltd.

said long ago, 'the most notable modern result of Percy's *Reliques of Ancient English Poetry'.* The success of Bishop Thomas Percy's *Reliques,* a collection of ballads, sonnets, historical songs and metrical romances, was truly astounding. Based on a seventeenth-century manuscript (now known as the 'Percy Folio'), the *Reliques,* first published in 1765, and revised and augmented in three subsequent editions before the end of the century (1767, 1775, 1794), was largely responsible for the eighteenth- and nineteenth-century revival of interest in older English and Scottish poetry. The highly charged dramatic simplicity and the 'romantic' flavour of such poems as 'The Ancient Ballad of Chevy Chase' fired the imaginations of generations of poets, from [Thomas] Chatterton and [William] Shenstone to D.G. Rossetti, [Algernon Charles] Swinburne, and beyond. During the Romantic period the 'popular' or 'traditional' ballad (as distinct from the 'broadside' ballad favoured by Wordsworth in the *Lyrical Ballads)* was very much in vogue—witness Sir Walter Scott's many imitations of the genre—and occasionally, as in 'The Ancient Mariner' and [John] Keats's 'La Belle Dame Sans Merci', the traditional ballad-form is utterly transformed by the intensely individual melody of true genius. 'The Ancient Mariner', it should be added, is not Coleridge's only early attempt in the genre: in the spring and summer of 1798 he began work on 'The Three Graves', 'The Ballad of the Dark Ladié', and, as well, on 'Christabel', which, while not a ballad *per se,* was influenced considerably by the ballad of 'Sir Cauline' in Percy's *Reliques.*

THE INSPIRATION OF 'SIR PATRICK SPENCE'

Coleridge's achievement in 'The Ancient Mariner', in terms both of indebtedness to tradition and of departure from it, can properly be appreciated only when one has a clear idea of the narrative and metrical characteristics of the ballads from which he drew his inspiration. Percy's ballad of 'Sir Patrick Spence', which Coleridge later used in his epigraph to 'Dejection: An Ode' (1802), is fortunately both representative and short enough to be given in full:

> The king sits in Dumferling toune,
>   Drinking the blude-reid wine:
> O quhar will I get guid sailòr,
>   To sail this ship of mine?

> Up and spak an eldern knicht,

Sat at the kings richt kne:
Sir Patrick Spence is the best sailòr,
    That sails upon the se.

The king has written a braid letter,
    And signd it wi' his hand;
And sent it to Sir Patrick Spence,
    Was walking on the sand.

The first line that Sir Patrick red,
    A loud lauch lauched he:
The next line that Sir Patrick red,
    The teir blinded his ee.

O quha is this has don this deid,
    This ill deid don to me;
To send me out this time o'the yeir,
    To sail upon the se?

Mak hast, mak haste, my mirry men all,
    Our guid schip sails the morne.
O say na sae, my master deir,
    For I feir a deadlie storme.

Late late yestreen I saw the new moone
    Wi' the auld moone in hir arme;
And I feir, I feir, my deir mastèr,
    That we will com to harme.

O our Scots nobles wer richt laith
    To weet their cork-heild schoone;
Bot lang owre a' the play wer playd,
    Thair hats they swam aboone.

O lang, lang, may thair ladies sit
    Wi' thair fans into their hand,
Or eir they se Sir Patrick Spence
    Cum sailing to the land.

O lang, lang, may the ladies stand
    Wi' thair gold kems in their hair,
Waiting for thair ain deir lords,
    For they'll se thame na mair.

Have owre, have owre to Aberdour,
    It's fiftie fadom deip:
And thair lies guid Sir Patrick Spence,
    Wi' the Scots lords at his feit. . . .

As in most traditional ballads, the language is plain and formulaic, there is no effort to describe the setting or delineate the characters, or to probe their psychological motivation, and little or no attempt is made to connect individual scenes or to describe the catastrophe which is the climax of the action. [As critic Anne H. Ehrenpreis remarks]:

The ballad's method of narration has been aptly compared to the film technique of montage: the story is advanced by a series of quick flashes, one distinct scene following another. There is no connecting tissue between the scenes, no explanation of events leading up to the crucial situation or following it.

'Sir Patrick Spence', like most folk ballads, focuses on a single episode, narrated by a detached commentator with stark economy but high dramatic intensity and immediacy. Its view of life is decidedly unsentimental, almost deterministic; and it can convey in the briefest of strokes vivid moments of love or of tragic loss. More than most other kinds of poetry, the ballad is capable of fulfilling the Miltonic dictum that poetry should be simple, sensuous and passionate; and 'I must only caution the Reader', as [poet Joseph] Addison said of the ballad of 'Chevy Chase', 'not to let the Simplicity of the Stile, which one may well pardon in so old a Poet, prejudice him against the Greatness of the Thought.'

SUPERNATURAL ELEMENTS IN BALLADS

One of the most prominent features of 'The Ancient Mariner', however, appears only sparingly in early ballads—namely, the supernatural. Although there are occasional ghosts in the folk ballads, they are harmless creatures, whose task is to admonish rather than to terrify the living. Certainly, there is nothing in traditional balladry to rival Coleridge's Polar Spirit or the graphic horror of such a nightmare spectre as Life-in-Death. The inspiration for such figures came from the literary horror-ballads of the eighteenth century, perhaps the best-known of which is [Gotfried August] Bürger's 'Lenore'. By comparison with 'The Ancient Mariner', Bürger's poem strikes the modern reader as tame and contrived; but there is no doubt that, in its time, it was sensational enough: 'Have you read the Balad call'd "Leonora"', enquired [Charles] Lamb with horrified delight in July 1796, 'in the 2d No. of the "Monthly Magazine"? —. If you have—!!!!!!!!!!!!!!!.'

'Lenore', which appeared in no less than seven English versions (one of them by Walter Scott) in 1796 alone, is the tale of Lenore's immoderate grief over the death of her lover Wilhelm, of Wilhelm's sudden appearance on horseback, and the elopement of the two lovers on an unearthly midnight ride. . . .

There were many other ballads, both translated from the German and English originals, that exploited the contemporary fashion and taste for the supernatural. M.G. Lewis's

'Alonzo the Brave and Fair Imogine' (1796), a Gothic ballad which Coleridge both knew and admired, carried the horrific to bizarre heights. . . .

Like Bürger's 'Lenore' and Lewis's 'Alonzo the Brave', 'The Ancient Mariner' is an imitation, with Gothic additions, of the traditional folk-ballad. At one level, then, it is admittedly derivative, drawing consciously upon earlier models—especially the ballads in Percy's *Reliques*—for much that is characteristic in its form and flavour. It owes a good deal, too, to the contemporary imitations of Bürger, Lewis and others: supernatural machinery, frequent use of internal rhyme, antiquated spelling and archaic diction, and so on. Whatever its debts to the ballad-tradition, however, 'The Ancient Mariner' is, as generations of critics have argued, more richly complex thematically and a more highly wrought technical accomplishment than any ballad written before or since. It is 'the acknowledged *chef d'oeuvre* [masterpiece] of the whole genre'.

Unlike Bürger and Lewis, Coleridge employs supernatural beings not for the gratuitous effects of *terror gratia terroris* [scary for the sake of being scary] but in order to project symbolically states and moods of the Mariner's inner being. The spectral figures are organic and functional, therefore, and not merely shocking and decoratively macabre; they are the leering and accusing incarnations of his own guilt and remorse, whom the Mariner confronts on his journey into the mirror and out again.

SOPHISTICATED USE OF LANGUAGE

Leaving character and theme aside, however, it is equally apparent that there is nothing comparable in earlier ballads to the sophisticated technical virtuosity of 'The Ancient Mariner'. Working with the traditional ballad-stanza, for example, Coleridge is able to achieve almost miraculous effects with the usual rhetorical devices of alliteration, internal rhyme, and repetition—as in the memorable account in Part II of the becalming of the Mariner's ship:

> The fair breeze blew, the white foam flew,
> The furrow followed free;
> We were the first that ever burst
> Into that silent sea.
>
> Down dropt the breeze, the sails dropt down,
> 'Twas sad as sad could be;

And we did speak only to break
The silence of the sea!

All in a hot and copper sky,
The bloody Sun, at noon,
Right up above the mast did stand,
No bigger than the Moon.

Day after day, day after day,
We stuck, nor breath nor motion;
As idle as a painted ship
Upon a painted ocean.

Water, water, every where,
And all the boards did shrink;
Water, water, every where,
Nor any drop to drink.

The very deep did rot: O Christ!
That ever this should be!
Yea, slimy things did crawl with legs
Upon the slimy sea.

About, about, in reel and rout
The death-fires danced at night;
The water, like a witch's oils,
Burnt green, and blue and white.

And some in dreams assuréd were
Of the Spirit that plagued us so;
Nine fathom deep he had followed us
From the land of mist and snow.

(103–34)

In these thirty-two lines there are twelve significant (sometime multiple) instances of alliteration, three striking examples of internal rhyme, and six major instances of verbal repetition. But what makes the passage so impressive is not its accumulation of such devices but rather the subtle and effective way in which rhetorical invention is varied and modulated—and the artful way in which it subserves a narrative end. Tumbled joyfully into the Pacific Ocean on a gust of rhyme and alliteration, the ship falls in the second stanza into the immobilising grip of an ocean-calm, and the torpor that afflicts body and soul is reflected in the phasing out of rhetorical effects in stanzas 2 and 3: alliteration drops off and then disappears entirely; the strong rhythm and internal rhymes of the opening stanza fall with the wind, leaving only the 'sight'-rhyme of 'speak'-'break' (line 109) as the tacit vestige of former activity; and the quick-paced assonance of the ship running before the breeze, overwhelmed by a series of long *o*-vowels, grows torpid and heavy under the influence of the fixed tropical sun. In stanzas 4 and 5, where the tedium of inertia is reinforced in languorous repetitions, there are also the beginnings of a countermovement—a quickening of the pulse that grows, paradoxically, out of these very repetitions. The calm begins, through repetition to evoke an emotional response and to acquire, as a result, a vitality of its own: lassitude (stanza 4) gives way to anguish (stanza 5), which, in its turn, prompts revulsion (stanza 6) that is transformed into an unconscious admiration of the calm's bewitching beauty (stanza 7). Thus, although the deadly calm maintains its hold on the Mariner's body, he experiences internally an emotional awakening, which builds through a crescendo of repetition and returning alliteration, and which opens out suddenly in the last two stanzas into an ominous universe governed by spirits of the air and water. In these eight stanzas, then, Coleridge suspends our disbelief and transports us in the Mariner's wake from the world of ordinary ships and men into the mysterious realm of the subconscious where the Polar Spirit dwells—and he accomplishes this, it must be stressed, within the framework of the traditional ballad-stanza and with the tools (for the most part) of traditional balladry.

EXPANDING BEYOND TRADITIONAL BALLADS

But the technical brilliance of 'The Ancient Mariner' does not depend only on Coleridge's manipulation of traditional forms and devices. There is an important measure of innovation as well. For illustration, one need look no further than his use of the ballad-stanza itself. While most ballads employ the customary four-line stanza used throughout 'Sir Patrick Spence' and Taylor's translation of Bürger's 'Lenore', Coleridge often relieves the monotony of this measure by extending his stanzas to five or six (and in one case nine) lines. Such expansion, which is more frequent in the supernatural parts of the story, serves a variety of functions. Sometimes it is used to heighten the emotional impact of an incident by drawing out its dramatic quality:

> With throats unslaked, with black lips baked,
> We could nor laugh nor wail;
> Through utter drought all dumb we stood!
> I bit my arm, I sucked the blood,
> And cried, A sail! a sail!

(157–61)

Sometimes, as in the case of the sailors' contradictory responses to the Mariner's deed, expansion by incremental repetition is used to fix a scene in the memory:

> And I had done a hellish thing,
> And it would work 'em woe:
> For all averred, I had killed the bird
> That made the breeze to blow.
> Ah wretch! said they, the bird to slay,
> That made the breeze to blow!
>
> Nor dim nor red, like God's own head,
> The glorious Sun uprist:
> Then all averred, I had killed the bird
> That brought the fog and mist.
> 'Twas right, said they, such birds to slay,
> That bring the fog and mist.

(91–102)

And sometimes expansion provides the means of intensifying a moment of lyric impulse, as when the 'troop of spirits blest' in Part V raise their matin hymn:

> Around, around, flew each sweet sound,
> Then darted to the Sun;
> Slowly the sounds came back again,
> Now mixed, now one by one.
>
> Sometimes a-dropping from the sky
> I heard the sky-lark sing;
> Sometimes all little birds that are,
> How they seemed to fill the sea and air
> With their sweet jargoning!
>
> And now 'twas like all instruments,
> Now like a lonely flute;
> And now it is an angel's song,
> That makes the heavens be mute.
>
> It ceased; yet still the sails made on
> A pleasant noise till noon,
> A noise like of a hidden brook
> In the leafy month of June,
> That to the sleeping woods all night
> Singeth a quiet tune.

(354–72)

The stanzas just quoted illustrate forcefully what is perhaps the major difference between 'The Ancient Mariner' and the traditional ballads on which it is modelled. One has only to compare the terse narrative and stark economy of imagery in such a poem as 'Sir Patrick Spence' to be immediately aware of the lyric and pictorial elaborateness of Coleridge's poem. While the anonymous medieval bard stresses action and situation almost to the exclusion of transition and explanation, Coleridge throws the emphasis onto the intricate elaboration of atmosphere, the careful description of time and setting, and the significance of moral edification in the narrative progression. In an intensely personal way he reworks the forms and rhetorical techniques of the old ballads and polishes them to a Regency[1] brilliance. Archaic diction (drawn from Chaucer and Spenser as well as from ballad tradition), alliteration, repetition and the ballad-stanza itself are all brought to maturity in 'The Ancient Mariner' and made to support the moral pattern of sin and expiation that lies at the heart of the poem. Similarly, the crude superstitious animism of the typical medieval ballad, like the gratuitously horrific supernatural of the later ballads of the Gothic revival, is spiritualised, internalised, and transformed into a powerful imaginative instrument to probe the dark recesses of the Mariner's troubled psyche. Unlike 'Sir Patrick Spence' or Bürger's 'Lenore', which are tales of deeds and actions, 'The Ancient Mariner' is in the final analysis a poem of the inner life. For all its affinities with earlier ballads, Coleridge's poem remains a work apart—a psychological ballad, a moral ballad, and (not to be forgotten) a lyrical ballad.

---

1. The period in England from 1811 to 1820 is called the Regency because King George III's eldest son, the Prince Regent, ruled the country. Although George was not dead, he had gone insane and blind, which led to this transfer of power.

A Critique of the Byronic Hero in *Manfred*

Andrew Rutherford

One of the archetypes of Romantic poetry is the Byronic hero, a stereotyped character common to the works of Lord George Gordon Byron. The typical Byronic hero is a tortured soul living in remorse over past sins, yet defiantly carrying on. Critics have often considered the title character of Byron's romantic drama *Manfred* as just such a hero, and readers have idealized Manfred as representing the nobility of the Romantic struggle against fate. Andrew Rutherford, however, contends that Byron's efforts to convincingly present Manfred as a defiant and exemplary Byronic hero are unconvincing and contradictory. In Rutherford's view, the key contradiction is that Byron wants Manfred to be seen as a man who is both doomed to his fate and yet able to make his own decisions. Rutherford is also critical of how Byron does not state explicitly many of Manfred's objectionable qualities, or past sins, leaving readers unclear of what tortures this lonely soul. Lacking this background, Manfred's anguish seems more petulant than noble. Instead of being a man who should be emulated, Manfred—in Rutherford's view—is a flawed and immature man whose superior character is not readily apparent in the poem. Rutherford concludes that other Byronic heroes, such as Childe Harold, are similarly imperfect and should be criticized for their actions instead of being viewed as heroic. Rutherford is the editor of *Byron: Augustan and Romantic* and the author of *Byron: A Critical Study*, the source of this article.

Excerpted from Andrew Rutherford, *Byron: A Critical Study*. Copyright © 1961 Stanford University Press. Reprinted with permission from Nancy M. Rutherford.

Formally, *Manfred* is a new departure for Byron—an experiment in semi-lyrical romantic drama, which derives from [Johann Wolfgang von] Goethe's *Faust*; but its content is familiar to a reader of *Childe Harold* and the verse tales. *Manfred* expresses, through a new set of conventions, Byron's own familiar notions, his own *Weltanschauung* [cultural view of the world], and Goethe was one of the first to acknowledge that the work was of completely different import from *his* masterpiece. It was only the failure of some readers to perceive this difference, and their talk of plagiarism, that made Byron once deny indignantly that he had used the German or the English Faustus. Normally he would admit quite readily that he had known the former, though he claimed it was of limited importance in the composition of his own poem:

> [Goethe's] *Faust* I never read [he told John Murray], for I don't
> know German; but Matthew Monk Lewis . . . at Coligny,
> translated most of it to me *vivâ voce* [out loud], and I was naturally much struck with it; but it was the *Staubach* and the
> *Fungfrau* and something else, much more than Faustus, that
> made me write *Manfred*. The first Scene, however, and that of
> Faustus are very similar.

INSPIRATIONS

His repeated emphasis on the part played by Alpine scenery is borne out by the work, for many passages of natural description echo phrases from his journal to [his sister] Augusta; yet this hardly provides an adequate account of the poem's genesis, far less its meaning. Byron's interest, after all, lies primarily in the hero, not the landscapes: they provide an appropriate setting for the action, but remain subordinate to the play's main purpose of displaying Manfred's character and problems. It was therefore disingenuous on Byron's part to say that he wrote it "for the sake of introducing the Alpine scenery in description," or that the "Journal . . . of my journey in the Alps . . . contains all the germs of *Manfred*"; yet this last remark comes nearer to the truth, since his journal was a record of his states of mind as well as of his travels and surroundings:

> In the weather for this tour (of 13 days), I have been very fortunate—fortunate in a companion (Mr. He.)—fortunate in our
> prospects, and exempt from even the little petty accidents and
> delays which often render journeys in a less wild country disappointing. I was disposed to be pleased. I am a lover of Na-

ture and an admirer of Beauty. I can bear fatigue and welcome privation, and have seen some of the noblest views in the world. But in all this—the recollections of bitterness, and more especially of recent and more home desolation, which must accompany me through life, have preyed upon me here; and neither the music of the Shepherd, the crashing of the Avalanche, nor the torrent, the mountain, the Glacier, the Forest, nor the Cloud, have for one moment lightened the weight upon my heart, nor enabled me to lose my own wretched identity in the majesty, and the power, and the Glory, around, above, and beneath me.

In its rather histrionic insistence on the intensity of his sufferings, and on the inefficacy of Nature as a cure, this passage is clearly related to the mood of *Manfred*. As one might expect, Byron's own feelings are the ultimate source for the poem—the "something else" which made him write it was presumably his recent history—not his domestic circumstances this time, but his relations, real or imagined, with Augusta, and their psychological aftermath. Incestuous guilt, or at least the idea of such guilt, seems to have been the mainspring of his inspiration, and if there are parallels with [François Auguste René Chateaubriand's] *René* and [Horace Walpole's] *The Mysterious Mother* it is probably because their themes chimed with his own preoccupations; and its basis in his own life was perhaps the reason for his trying to divert attention to more incidental "sources" like the Alpine scenery.

Lord George Gordon Byron

Manfred is not, however, autobiographical, nor does it stand in the fairly close relation that *Childe Harold* does to Byron's own experience. He draws on his life (and reading) only to create a work of more general significance, a fantastic drama of the supernatural which will embody his ideal of human greatness. Here more than in any other poem we see him as a maker of myths, and the play is in an important sense the culmination of his whole romantic phase, since it is his supreme attempt to claim significance and value for the character of the Byronic hero. . . .

A Contradictory Hero

Although Byron himself described it as "inexplicable," his general intention is quite clear: as E.H. Coleridge observes "the *motif* of *Manfred* is remorse—eternal suffering for inexpiable crime," and the play consists of a progressive revelation of the hero's character and history, and of the stages in his search for an escape from guilt.

In the opening scene Manfred appears at midnight in a Gothic gallery, to soliloquise about his mental torment, and to invoke the Spirits of Earth, Ocean, Air, Night, Mountains, Winds, and his own Star. They come in answer to his final summons, which expresses his sense of fatality—of being under a curse, and this idea is developed by the Seventh Spirit's first speech:

> The Star which rules thy destiny
> Was ruled, ere earth began, by me:
> It was a World as fresh and fair
> As e'er revolved round Sun in air;
> Its course was free and regular,
> Space bosomed not a lovelier star.
> The Hour arrived—and it became
> A wandering mass of shapeless flame,
> A pathless Comet, and a curse,
> The menace of the Universe;
> Still rolling on with innate force,
> Without a sphere, without a course,
> A bright deformity on high,
> The monster of the upper sky!
> And Thou! beneath its influence born—
> Thou worm! whom I obey and scorn—
> Forced by a Power (which is not thine,
> And lent thee but to make thee mine)
> For this brief moment to descend
> Where these weak Spirits round thee bend
> And parley with a thing like thee—
> What would'st thou, Child of Clay! with me?

These lines are much better than the jingles sung or spoken by the other Spirits. Byron is writing about something which he really felt and imagined vividly—he has returned with new power to the conception of a noble nature doomed by some fate, blasted, and perverted from Promethean[1] potentialities to almost Satanic evil. It is difficult, however, to say precisely what this passage means in terms of the play's ac-

---

1. Refers to the Titan Prometheus, who in Greek mythology was punished by the god Zeus for having given fire to mankind. Later myths say that Prometheus created humans.

tion. If this Spirit rules the star under which Manfred was born, has he controlled or influenced the hero's life? Was it he, or some external Fate, who was responsible for the dire change in the star, and was this change the cause of Man-

---

BYRON IDENTIFIES WITH HIS POETIC HEROES

Lord Byron sought to identify with the heroes he created, including Don Juan. Preeminent Byron scholar Leslie A. Marchand examines how Byron tries to parallel his life with that of the legendary Lothario. Marchand concludes that while Byron identifies with Don Juan, the character is rather flat and less revealing than other heroes such as Manfred.

Byron took delight in creating a Don Juan who was not a heartless pursuer and despoiler of women like the legendary character, but a gentle innocent, first seduced by the self-deluding Donna Julia, then engulfed in the "natural love" of the sinless Haidée, repelled and revolted by the imperious commands of the Sultan's favorite, Gulbeyez, who had bought him for her pleasure, passively accepting the caresses of the supple Dudù, essentially unchanged at being swept by cir-cumstances into the position of favorite of Catherine the Great (though Byron allows us to assume that he was becoming more *gâté* and *blasé* as he grew in experience), and finally be-coming a detached observer of the intrigues and hypocrisies of the English society into which he was thrown in the last cantos, but ending on the solid breast of "her frolic Grace," the Duchess of Fitz-Fulke.

In general this follows Byron's own concept of his relations with women. Reputed to be a rake and a seducer, he felt him-self the most pursued of men. Replying to a distorted story of his abduction of the Countess Guiccioli, he wrote: "I should like to know *who* has been carried off—except poor dear *me*. I have been more ravished myself than any body since the Trojan war. . . ."

But Byron's identification with the character he had created for the poem was far from complete; in fact, Don Juan scarcely develops as a personality, for Byron was content to use him as a pawn, a kind of simple norm against which to view the irrationality of the world. So that as a character re-flecting striking and recognizable Byronic traits he is much less revealing than the heroes of many of Byron's less realistic poems—the Corsair or Manfred, for example.

Leslie A. Marchand, *Byron's Poetry: A Critical Introduction.* Boston: Houghton Mifflin, 1965.

fred's sin? Or was "the Hour" not predetermined by any agency, supernatural or astrological? Was it simply the hour of sin, committed of the hero's own accord, and is the change in the star a mere symbolical description of the change in Manfred's soul? These questions are unanswered and unanswerable, so that there is a serious confusion or obscurity in the play's metaphysics, and these are still further complicated by the Spirit's later comments which suggest a devil trying to win the hero's soul. Byron is using some ideas that fascinated him, and expressing them well enough to give us an agreeable *frisson* of horror, but he does not seem to have defined them clearly even to himself, or to have worked them into a coherent system, even in this one poem. There is, indeed, an almost wilful confusion on the question of Free Will *versus* Predestination, and this enables him to have it both ways: Manfred has all the glamour which in Byron's eyes attached itself to a doomed hero, "fatal and fated in [his] sufferings"; but he is also shown as a kind of superman, choosing his own course in defiance of all supernatural powers, and the contradiction is never examined or resolved.

There is a less important ambiguity about the status of the other Spirits. Byron may be writing allegorically, in which case they represent aspects of physical Nature, or he may be suggesting, through this new mythology, some spiritual life behind natural phenomena; but the basic interpretation of the scene would be the same in either case. Manfred asks these Spirits for "forgetfulness," though the cause of his unrest is still a secret. They reply that they can give him mastery of the elements which are under their control, but that they have no power to grant oblivion; and as they are immortal, they cannot tell him whether death will bring what he desires. Here Byron seems to be rejecting the Wordsworthian and Shelleyan notions of *Childe Harold*, Canto III: he is denying the power of Nature (physical or spiritual) to minister to a mind diseased, or to provide a haven for the disembodied soul.

ARTISTIC SLEIGHT OF HAND

Towards the end of the scene the Seventh Spirit rather maliciously assumes the form of "a beautiful female figure," and from Manfred's frenzied outburst we deduce that it was that of his lost love (Astarte). The Incantation which follows, spoken presumably by this spirit or the lady, adds to our sense of mystification, but fills out our picture of the hero as a man accursed and sinful, isolated from his fellows by his agony and guilt:

> By thy cold breast and serpent smile,
> By thy unfathomed gulfs of guile,
> By that most seeming virtuous eye,
> By thy shut soul's hypocrisy;
> By the perfection of thine art
> Which passed for human thine own heart;
> By thy delight in others' pain,
> And by thy brotherhood of Cain,
> I call upon thee! and compel
> Thyself to be thy proper Hell!

Many of the faults, however, which are thus attributed to Manfred, are not shown in his soliloquies or actions in the play, and this would seem to be another case of Byron "having it both ways." All his heroes in the early verse tales had been paradoxical mixtures of good and evil, vice and virtue, but their more unpleasant crimes were never fully presented in the poems, so that the reader—like the author—could enjoy the romantic villainy without ever facing its real implications. Something of the same kind happens now in *Manfred*, for the hero's sinful past is emphasised to make him seem more interesting and awe-inspiring, but the more objectionable qualities (like hypocrisy or delight in others' pain) are excluded from the actual portrayal of his character, by an artistic sleight of hand amounting to dishonesty. . . .

Manfred Is Not a Champion of Mankind

Manfred is not in any sense a representative or champion of Mankind. Byron was undoubtedly attracted by the notion of a hero who, though greater than his fellows in both rank and genius, none the less devotes himself to their cause, and Prometheus provided him with a prototype which was often in his mind that summer. Yet this conception does not affect Manfred—he shows pity and consideration for the human beings whom he despises, but he is not interested in bettering their lot. In his youth he had had "noble aspirations" of this kind:

> To make my own the mind of other men,
> The enlightener of nations . . .

but in reality he shrank from all contact with men, even as their leader and benefactor:

I could not tame my nature down; for he
Must serve who fain would sway; and soothe, and sue,
And watch all time, and pry into all place,
And be a living Lie, who would become
A mighty thing amongst the mean—and such
The mass are; I disdained to mingle with
A herd, though to be leader—and of wolves.
The lion is alone and so am I.

It is tempting to contrast this with the unfailing common sense and patience with which Byron managed the dishonest, quarrelsome, unreliable Greeks at Missolonghi[2]—he himself, in that last chapter of his life, provides us with a standard by which Manfred's bombast can be judged and found contemptible—by which Manfred himself is seen to be sadly defective as an ideal. But quite apart from this question of the value and propriety of the hero's attitudes, it is clear that he is no Prometheus but a Prometheus *manqué* [unfulfilled, lacking], and that although he defies supernatural powers this does not affect the material or spiritual condition of mankind. His is an entirely private martyrdom, and he cannot be said to represent humanity or the mind of man—he is an exceptional, unique phenomenon, his problems are peculiar to himself, and their solution (if there is one) has no bearing on the situation of *nous autres* [the rest of us].

This difference between Men and Manfred is insisted on throughout the poem, yet one is never quite persuaded of its truth. Here, as in almost all of his "romantic" works, Byron seems to demand more sympathy and admiration for the hero than he shows him to deserve. We are always hearing about Manfred's greatness, for not only do we have his own descriptions of himself, but almost every character acts as a foil or as a chorus voicing some kind of awed respect and praise. Yet his superiority is a matter of repeated assertion rather than convincing demonstration. All the posturings of pride and defiance, all the nursing of his melancholy and misanthropy, all the clamouring about his love and agony, do not make him an impressive or a tragic figure: there is little or no advance on the morality and characterisation of *The Giaour*, for Byron is absorbed with the same vision of a noble and passionate lover blasted by sins, racked by remorse and grief, but defying everyone and everything. The only dif-

2. Missolonghi is the town in Greece where Byron died on April 19, 1824. He had gone to Greece to help organize the country's revolt against Turkish rule.

ference is that Manfred is portrayed more fully, and an attempt is made to read deeper significance into his favourite attitudes and feelings, but the effect of this is to make us realise more clearly than ever before the faults and limitations of this hero-type, and its inadequacy for the role imposed upon it here. The treatment of the central problem of guilt, to take one crucial aspect of the work, consists of triviality masquerading as grandeur: just as in *The Giaour,* Byron distinguishes between repentance and remorse only so that the hero can reject the former, which he sees as an indignity, to wallow in the latter. This new spiritual superman, in fact, has an emotional and intellectual immaturity of a kind usually associated with adolescence, and while this would not have mattered so much in a verse-tale entertainment, it is fatally disabling in a moral-metaphysical play like *Manfred.* The more seriously we are asked to take the hero, the more serious must be our criticism of his defects; and the more we study him and his career, the more we see the truth of [T.S.] Eliot's comment that "It is . . . impossible to make out of [Byron's] diabolism anything coherent or rational."

The Power of Nature in Shelley's "Ode to the West Wind"

Harold Bloom

In the following article, Harold Bloom considers the depiction of nature in Percy Bysshe Shelley's "Ode to the West Wind." Shelley praises the power of nature and expresses his desire to become part of it. The wind is described as both a destructive force and a sign that spring, renewal, and imagination will return. Shelley's love of the wind is religious—he prays to the wind to let him experience its power, like a leaf or a cloud might. Bloom is a prominent literary critic and the Sterling Professor of the Humanities at Yale University. His works include *Western Canon: The Books and School of the Ages.*

With [*Ode to the West Wind*] we move . . . to the autumn of 1819, when [Percy Bysshe Shelley] had finished the first three acts of *Prometheus Unbound* but before he had added the astonishing afterthought of the fourth (October 1819). The tentative mythmaking apprehensions of the poems of 1816 have now been confirmed, and Shelley sees himself as the prophet of a rising wind which heralds destruction of an old world and creation of a new. He raises his psalm to the glory of what is coming, and as a celebration of much that departs.

Seasonal Cycles

Shelley's note to his ode places the circumstances of its composition. In a wood that skirts the Arno, near Florence, on a day when the wind is rising and collecting the vapors that pour down the autumnal rains, the poet at sunset observes the turning of the year, the passage into fall. As the night comes on, a violent tempest of hail and rain descends. In this autumnal advent the poet reads the signs of a creative de-

Excerpted from Harold Bloom, *The Visionary Company: A Reading of English Romantic Poetry*, revised edition. Copyright © 1971 Cornell University. Reprinted with permission from the publisher, Cornell University Press.

struction that will affect the whole condition of man. Even as the destroying westerly wind now sweeps toward the winter of the world, so another wind from the same quarter will bring in the spring the following year. But though the poem salutes the second wind ("thine azure sister of the Spring"), it concerns itself not with cycle but with the possibility of breaking out of cycle into a spring that shall not pass away:

> O wild West Wind, thou breath of Autumn's being,
> Thou from whose unseen presence the leaves dead
> Are driven, like ghosts from an enchanter fleeing,
>
> Yellow, and black, and pale, and hectic red,
> Pestilence-stricken multitudes! O thou
> Who chariotest to their dark wintry bed
>
> The wingèd seeds, where they lie cold and low,
> Each like a corpse within its grave, until
> Thine azure sister of the Spring shall blow
>
> Her clarion o'er the dreaming earth, and fill
> (Driving sweet buds like flocks to feed in air)
> With living hues and odours plain and hill;
>
> Wild Spirit, which art moving everywhere;
> Destroyer and preserver; hear, oh, hear!

The wind, like the Beauty of the *Hymn*, is an "unseen presence." Before this presence's exorcising enchantment the dead leaves flee to their necessary destruction, but the live seeds are "charioted" to the salvation of a winter's sleep, akin to that of the sleepers who will awake into resurrection. The spring wind is a shepherdess of a renewed pastoral innocence, whose clarion of judgment will awaken earth to renewal. The stanza ends with a confronting call to the wind to hear its prophet. This pattern is repeated in the second and third stanzas, which also end in summoning the wind to heed the poet's prayer. In the first stanza, observing the wind's effect upon the forest, Shelley sees the dead leaves driven along beneath tangled boughs still covered with leaves. In the second he transfers his gaze to the sky:

> Thou on whose stream, mid the steep sky's commotion,
> Loose clouds like earth's decaying leaves are shed,
> Shook from the tangled boughs of Heaven and Ocean,
>
> Angels of rain and lightning! there are spread
> On the blue surface of thine aëry surge,
> Like the bright hair uplifted from the head
>
> Of some fierce Maenad, even from the dim verge
> Of the horizon to the zenith's height,

The locks of the approaching storm. Thou dirge

Of the dying year, to which this closing night
Will be the dome of a vast sepulchre,
Vaulted with all thy congregated might

Of vapours, from whose solid atmosphere
Black rain, and fire, and hail will burst: oh, hear!

THE DESTRUCTION OF PEACE AND BEAUTY

The tangled boughs of Heaven and Ocean are the higher, more stationary clouds; the loose clouds beneath them are driven by the wind, just as the dead leaves are driven below. The heavens, like the forest, are dying, and yielding their substance up to the destroying wind. As the wind sweeps on, the woods act as a vast aeolian lyre and give forth a dirgelike sound. The year and its dependent life are imprisoned in the sepulcher dominated by the blackening dome of the stormy evening sky, from which the black rain, fire, and hail of destruction will burst. The figure of black rain has in it a hint of revolution, and reminds us that Shelley is heralding also an overthrow of the age of Metternich and Castlereagh.[1]

What is destroyed in the third stanza is a natural peace and beauty, which scarcely needs the fierce destructive grace of the abolishing wind. The sweep of apocalypse carries away the best of old order as well as what needs burial:

Thou who didst waken from his summer dreams
The blue Mediterranean, where he lay,
Lulled by the coil of his crystàlline streams,

Beside a pumice isle in Baiae's bay,
And saw in sleep old palaces and towers
Quivering within the wave's intenser day,

All overgrown with azure moss, and flowers
So sweet, the sense faints picturing them! Thou
For whose path the Atlantic's level powers

Cleave themselves into chasms, while far below
The sea-blooms and the oozy woods which wear
The sapless foliage of the ocean, know

Thy voice, and suddenly grow gray with fear,
And tremble and despoil themselves: oh, hear!

Azure is Shelley's color for the triumphant joy of imagi-

1. Prince Klemems von Metternich was an Austrian statesman and minister of foreign affairs. Viscount Robert Stewart Castlereagh was a British statesman who served in several early nineteenth-century cabinets. The conservative politics of these men, which included efforts to supress revolts, make them anathema to radicals such as Shelley.

nation made manifest in nature. He uses it to mean what is delicate, gracious, clear, pleasant, sometimes even without reference to color. The Mediterranean is only lulled, but the illusion of peace is itself an Elysian [paradisiacal] value, and Shelley laments its sacrifice to the wind. The "old palaces and towers," once tokens of tyranny, have been mellowed by time and receive their ultimate imaginative form by being reflected on the calm waters of the sea. This is the best that nature's own art can do with reality, and it is beautiful, but it cannot abide the intensity of the wind.

So far the poet himself has not entered his poem, but in the last two stanzas he replaces leaf, cloud, and wave as the object of the wind's force. The poem's meaning turns upon the deliberate contrast between the fourth and fifth stanzas. In the fourth the poet pleads for a negation of his human status; he wishes to be only an object for the wind, like leaf, cloud, wave. His despair here is like the despair of Job, who calls upon the wind to dissolve his substance. The final stanza recoils from this surrender, and cries out for a mutual relation with the wind. Yet even the Jobean fourth stanza is far removed from self-pity, modern critical opinion to the contrary:

> If I were a dead leaf thou mightest bear;
> If I were a swift cloud to fly with thee;
> A wave to pant beneath thy power, and share
>
> The impulse of thy strength, only less free
> Than thou, O uncontrollable! If even
> I were as in my boyhood, and could be
>
> The comrade of thy wanderings over Heaven,
> As then, when to outstrip thy skiey speed
> Scarce seemed a vision; I would ne'er have striven
>
> As thus with thee in prayer in my sore need.
> Oh, lift me as a wave, a leaf, a cloud!
> I fall upon the thorns of life! I bleed!
>
> A heavy weight of hours has chained and bowed
> One too like thee: tameless, and swift, and proud.

RELIGIOUS DESPAIR

If I were merely part of nature, or if I still possessed the imaginative strength of my boyhood, then I would not be striving with you now in prayer in my sore need. These lines mix a Wordsworthian plangency for the hiding places of imaginative power with the accents of wrestling Jacob, who

would not let the angel go until a divine blessing was be-
stowed. Yet this Jacob momentarily lets go in despair of his
struggle and, as a mere natural object, falls back, out of the
Spirit, and onto the thorns of life. Job, feeling his abandonment, cried out, "He hath cast me into the mire, and I am become like dust and ashes." A rhetorical critic could as justi-
fiably, and as inaptly, accuse Job of self-pity, as he does
Shelley. The *Ode to the West Wind*, like the Book of Job, is a
religious poem, and the conventions of religious rhetoric ap-
ply equally to each work. Shelley's song falters in the fourth
stanza with the deliberation of religious despair and the
pathos of the rejected and wasted prophet.

The last stanza of the *Hymn to Intellectual Beauty* echoed
the "sober coloring" of the last stanza of Wordsworth's *Intimations* ode by speaking of "a harmony in autumn, and a
lustre in its sky." Similarly, the final stanza of Shelley's
greatest ode modulates to "a deep, autumnal tone":

> Make me thy lyre, even as the forest is:
> What if my leaves are falling like its own!
> The tumult of thy mighty harmonies
>
> Will take from both a deep, autumnal tone,
> Sweet though in sadness. Be thou, Spirit fierce,
> My spirit! Be thou me, impetuous one!
>
> Drive my dead thoughts over the universe
> Like withered leaves to quicken a new birth!
> And, by the incantation of this verse,
>
> Scatter, as from an unextinguished hearth
> Ashes and sparks, my words among mankind!
> Be through my lips to unawakened earth
>
> The trumpet of a prophecy! O Wind,
> If Winter comes, can Spring be far behind? . . .

THE POET'S MIND

The leaves are the poet's thoughts, falling dead to earth. But
these dead leaves fall, to be lifted again by the wind and to
be driven by it over the universe to quicken a new birth.
Quite humbly, Shelley is suggesting that his thoughts may be
useful to fertilize the age he wishes to stir into life. For his
poem, he claims more. The prayer to the wind stresses mutual need; if the prophet needs the divine, the divine as as-
suredly needs the prophet if the message is to be heard by
men. Shelley is praying for energy and life, and offers it rec-
ompense a human voice, to be the trumpet of a prophecy.

In his passionate prose essay *A Defence of Poetry* (1821), Shelley was to return to the figure of "an unextinguished hearth" as an emblem of his poetic mind: "The mind in creation is as a fading coal, which some invisible influence, like an inconstant wind, awakens to transitory brightness; this power arises from within, like the colour of a flower which fades and changes as it is developed."

The mind of Shelley, in creating his *Ode,* is such a coal or hearth, never quite faded, never altogether extinguished. The west wind awakens it to a transitory brightness, but the poem's color still comes from a power within the mind. The prophecy is Shelley's own, for it must pass through his lips if it is to reawaken man as well as earth, and his lips modify even as they sound forth the wind's song. With Isaiah the prophet, the agnostic poet of the *Ode to the West Wind* could have said that a live coal from the divine altar had touched his lips.

Medieval Influences in Keats's "La Belle Dame Sans Merci"

Stuart M. Sperry

During his brief life and career, John Keats wrote many famous odes, including "Ode to a Nightingale" and "Ode on a Grecian Urn." However, he also wrote medieval-style poems, such as "The Eve of St. Agnes" and "La Belle Dame Sans Merci." According to Stuart M. Sperry, "La Belle Dame Sans Merci" is the finest example of Keats's efforts in this vein. Keats is able to take the Celtic and Arthurian mythological influences and rework them to convey his own beliefs about the essence of poetry. In Keats's view, poetry turns common experience into enchantment, and thus the magic within the poem reflects Keats's larger worldview, bringing deeper meaning to this work. Sperry, who died in 1998, was Professor Emeritus of English at Indiana University in Bloomington.

Following the completion of *The Eve of St. Agnes* and his work on the fragmentary *Eve of Saint Mark,* Keats made one more attempt at a poem of a medieval character. However, "La Belle Dame" represents an infinitely more profound assimilation of the medieval spirit, or, more accurately perhaps, the transformation of that spirit within the terms of an essentially modern style and sensibility, than anything in the pseudogothicism of *St. Agnes* or the architectural background of *Saint Mark.* In many respects the poem represents the culmination of his absorption over a number of months with a variety of medieval styles and attitudes, a complex of possibilities that suddenly, perhaps in the course of a single evening, achieved a formal and thematic definition through a pressure of deeply felt and personal concerns.

SPENSERIAN INFLUENCES

Just as it remains impossible to limit those concerns to any single issue of his private life, so it is equally impossible to describe the medieval quality of his ballad of fairy enchantment and loss in terms of any single analogue, such as the ballad of "Thomas Rymer" or the story of *Sir Launfal* [by Thomas Chestre], however suggestive anyone of these may prove. Those critics who have repeatedly tried to explain the poem by means of any single source have generally concluded, despite occasional insights, with results as barren as the landscape that envelops Keats's knight. Undoubtedly [literary scholar] Douglas Bush is right that as regards imagery, phrasing, and general suggestiveness, [Edmund Spenser's] *The Faerie Queene* presents the closest parallels: not merely the episodes involving Cymochles and Phaedria and the False Florimel, but Duessa's seduction of the Red Cross Knight and, by significant contrast, "Arthur's wholly inspiring vision of the Faerie Queene." Yet to compare any one or all of these episodes with "La Belle Dame" is to sense immediately how much Keats has made contact with an ethos that lies very much in the background of Spenser's romance and on which the older poet drew throughout—the world of Arthurian legend and more particularly its source in Celtic lore. To feel, as every reader has, the elfin grace and cunning of Keats's fairy enchantress, the wild and touching beauty of her secret ways, is to feel how much the mystery and desolation of the poem transcend the patent villany of a Duessa or a Phaedria, how much closer we are to the ambivalence of such divinities as Rhiannon and Morrigan[1] and the heroes they alternately adopted and beguiled, a race of whom [Matthew] Arnold wrote, "the moment one goes below the surface,—almost before one goes below the surface,—all is illusion and phantasy, double-meaning, and far-reaching mythological import. . . . These are no mediaeval personages; they belong to an older, pagan, mythological world." There is no reason to imagine Keats was ever deeply versed in the whole of Arthurian legend or the folklore that informs so much of it, although the standard sources, such as [Thomas] Malory, were available to him, and there is evi-

---

1. In Welsh mythology, Rhiannon is a version of Epona, the horse-goddess, and the mistress of the Singing Birds. Morrigan is a goddess of strife, battle, and fertility in Celtic mythology.

dence that he became increasingly interested in the ballad and its lore during his walking tour into the north country, Scotland, and Ireland. It is simply characteristic of his genius that he was able, by a process of unconscious assimilation and in the brief space of forty-eight lines, to distill the essence of the magic that, as Arnold saw, pervades from its origins a whole current of English literature. It is in this larger sense that the poem is truly archetypal.

With all the swiftness of its narrative, its ballad-like compression, "La Belle Dame" owes much of its power both to an extraordinary clarity and to a suggestiveness of detail. The autumnal lake, the silent birds, the knight's pacing steed, the meal of strange forest fruits, and the sudden vision of the company of death-pale warriors and the dread name they utter: these and other details have the sharp distinctness and contraction of images remaining from a dream, as though they held the clue to a larger drama of partly hidden significance. The major subject of the narrative, the story of the fairy enchantress who comes from the other world to grant her love to a mortal, to destroy or to save him, is a stock feature of a multitude of Celtic lays [simple narrative poems] and Arthurian romances. "La Belle Dame" is remarkable for the way it achieves its peculiar effectiveness, the power actually of a kind of resonance, by analogy not with any single tale or romance but with the whole tradition of the fairy mistress as it has come down to us from any number of sources, a tradition whose details and implications Keats has developed in his own individual way. We find, for example, that the fairy enchantress is commonly represented throughout Celtic lore as an inhabitant of lakes and other bodies of water, a hyperborean, perhaps, but fundamentally related to the race of naiads who had fascinated him from the time of "Sleep and Poetry" and whom he had connected from the first with the mythological beginnings of poetry. Instead of "many a Nymph who wreaths her Brows with Sedge," however, we now see only withered reeds around a desolate lake. We find also that one of the manifestations of the fairy enchantress's power is the singing of the magic birds that often accompany her—the song, for example, of the enchanted birds that cast Cuchulinn[2] into sleep, or the music, as Arnold himself recalled, of "the birds

2. Cuchulinn is a hero-king and warlike figure in Celtic mythology.

of Rhiannon, whose song was so sweet that warriors remained spell-bound for eighty years together listening to them." Such melody is like the music of the Val des Faux Soulas in the romances, "a valley of surpassing loveliness, the home of singing birds, green and fresh even in mid-winter." This otherworldly paradise to which knights are lured by their fairy lovers, however, is closely akin, perhaps inseparable from, the Val sanz Retor, where the knight may be given the task of unspelling other, earlier captives but frequently is himself imprisoned forever in a curtain of druidic mist suggestive of the grave. It is the whole complex texture of these relationships, together with the note of ambivalence and foreboding of departed magic that surrounds them, that Keats's poem conveys and that we sense behind the simplicity of the refrain, "And no birds sing."

One should note, moreover, that the fairy goddess of Celtic lore, especially the divinity of lakes and streams, is not simply a baneful enchantress, luring knights to their doom. She is also, by a curious paradox, the nurturer and foster parent of heroes, the donor of precious gifts who instructs them in magic and the arts of prophecy. Among the most common of her gifts are a horse and a coat of arms. Thus La Dame du Lac gives a spirited white horse and a coat of arms to her hero, Lancelot. In a number of romances the fay appears to her lover riding a mysterious horse and takes him up with her, a relationship Keats appears to have reversed in his ballad. As scholars such as Roger Loomis have pointed out, however, La Dame du Lac, the benevolent fay, is in reality Morgan la Fée, the malevolent enchantress, in another guise; the two are parts of a larger duality and trace their ancestry to a common source. There is an obvious fatality in all this: the divinity who protects and instructs the hero fulfills her love by seducing and destroying him. In a similar way Keats's "elfin grot" corresponds to the cave where, time and again in Celtic story, the hero is lured by his enchantress and their relationship is, in one way or another, consummated. As Lucy Paton has shown, there is an evident connection between such Celtic material and the classical story of Endymion, the shepherd cast into dreaming slumber on the hillside by Diana. The hillside of classical legend becomes the cave of Celtic fable, closely associated with the funeral barrows of the dead (Keats actually has both cave and hillside in his ballad). Rather than a dream of heavenly love, however, the vision now becomes a journey to the underworld and a visit to the souls of the departed, a perilous adventure since it can result in perpetual imprisonment, as indeed Merlin is eternally bound by Niniane, the Celtic fay and dweller by the Lac du Dyane.

ELEMENTS OF NORTHERN MYTHOLOGY

Without a need for further particulars, one can see from a number of details that "La Belle Dame" is an original assimilation of a closely knit body of early northern legend, a network of stories connected more or less subterraneously with classical mythology and many of the themes that had been at the center of Keats's visionary preoccupations in *Endymion*. It is possible to account for his shift of interest from southern to northern mythology through the extraordinary complexity and ambivalence of so much Celtic legend, its darker coloring and Christian overtones, particularly its suggestions of the story of the Fall, an event that, in its various implications, had begun to haunt his imagination. Primarily, no doubt, it was the supremely enigmatic quality of the Celtic fay, together with her relevance to a complex of personal concerns, poetic and otherwise, that was most compelling. Summing up the nature of the Celtic goddess under the type of Morgan la Fée—"a female pantheon in miniature"—Loomis has described her in words that are worth quoting:

> She was a sort of naiad or nereid, haunting springs, rivers, fords, lakes, and seas, or dwelling beneath their surfaces; she was a foster-mother of heroes, who took them in their infancy, trained them for high adventure, and watched over them in peril; she showered wealth on her favorites; . . . she foretold the future; she was both a beneficent and a sinister power; she lay in wait for mortals, offering them her love; she possessed a very swift and powerful horse.

Some understanding of the Celtic fay and the extraordinary richness and ambivalence of her character provides important clues for the interpretation of "La Belle Dame." Thus it is clear that Keats's ballad is nothing so simple as a tale of guileful seduction and betrayal. Nor can it be taken purely in the opposite sense, as [Earl] Wasserman would have it—as the knight's initiation into the mysteries that lie beyond "heaven's bourne," a state of spiritual elevation that, through the fallibility of his mortal powers, he is unable to sustain. To some degree both sets of implication are present. Indeed it is the larger irony of the poem that it joins them inseparably.

POSITIVE AND NEGATIVE MAGIC

Such relationships can be seen most directly in the feast of strange fruits the maiden provides her lover prior to his sleep within her cave. Beginning with the realm of "Flora, and old Pan," with its "apples red, and strawberries" on which the youthful poet feeds, to the angelic meal of "summer fruits" in the *Fall of Hyperion,* a banquet Keats endows with sacramental overtones, the feast of fruits, like the suggestion of love-making that follows it in Keats's ballad, is the usual prelude to visionary experience. Like the apple, so common in Celtic story, by which the fay entices the lover to her domain, the strange roots and honey, the "manna dew" she offers him, are clearly symbolic of what anthropologists have for some time described as "mana," the magical power of transmuting or transcending external nature, Arnold's "natural magic," the transforming power of the poetic imagination.

Yet we know that "mana" is also "taboo": the two are one and the same, positive and negative aspects of a single power. Mana, that is to say, is magic taken as a sacred and creative energy; taboo is the same force considered in its terrifying and minatory, if not necessarily prohibitive, implications. It is notable that Celtic tales and later romances dealing with the fairy mistress make frequent use of the theme of the *ges* or taboo she places on her lover, suggestions of which cling to Keats's ballad. Thus, she sometimes forbids him to eat food on first entering her kingdom or after his return to the mortal world; more frequently she commands him, on leaving her, never to reveal her name. Within the condensed structure of Keats's ballad, the fruits she offers him clearly serve as mana and taboo in one, as an experience that is both initiatory and fateful, while the knight learns the name of his enchantress, the clue to her deeper identity, only in the dream of the starved warriors who have preceded him, only, that is, at the price of his own enslavement. One cannot dismiss the rites La Belle Dame lightly practices as mere deception; nor is the knight's dream the mere figment of a disordered imagination, a purely subjective response. Neither part of his narration, the "before" or the "after," is more believable or real than the other, for neither part has meaning without the other. The real significance of the events he relates lies in the irony of their juxta-position, in the terrifying incongruity between the endless staring faces of his vision and the casual charm and rapture of the brief encounter that occasioned it.

Like so much of Keats's other verse, "La Belle Dame" is most of all about the essence of poetry itself, the gift of that "natural magic" that transforms common experience into enchantment and later vision. It is a miniature allegory of the growth and development of the poetic consciousness dramatized through the details of the knight's relation and the great central themes of love, death, and immortality. What is remarkable about the poem within the larger canon of Keats's work is the perfect blend of pathos and irony it achieves by its compression and simplicity together with the range of its suggestiveness. It is almost a reworking in miniature of the romance between Endymion and Cynthia in darker, northern colors. It broaches the theme of fairy captivation to which Keats was to return in a more cynical and bitter way in *Lamia*. Nevertheless, we miss a further, major range of implication unless we see the ballad's rela-tionship to a later work to which it is rarely, if ever, com-pared: *The Fall of Hyperion*. For both poems deal with the growth of tragic knowledge and awareness from their first roots in mere sensuous enchantment, the fall from inno-cence into experience the muse of poetry inflicts, in her de-signingly capricious way, on those she favors most. Keats's fairy enchantress is also, in her darker guise, Fata Morgana, a role he was to seek to make endurable through the inter-vention and instruction of Moneta and by recasting the pa-gan fable into the form of a Christian allegory of divine re-demption. However, the realization "La Belle Dame" leaves with us is of a simpler but ultimately perhaps more truthful kind: the transience of bliss, the community of individual desires and dreams, the finality of death, and the eternal hunger for renewed experience even in the face of tragic awareness. If at the end Keats's knight seems blind to such conclusions, if he can only turn back to the fading landscape with words that are an inconsequence, that is only the cul-minating irony of the poem.

CHAPTER 3

Romantic Novelists and Essayists

Romantic and Anti-Romantic Elements in Scott's *Waverley*

Robin Mayhead

Robin Mayhead explains how Sir Walter Scott's novel *Waverley* can be characterized as both Romantic and anti-Romantic. According to Mayhead, Scott's use of wild scenery and supernatural elements link the writer to other Romantic poets and authors. However, Scott is set apart from his contemporaries because *Waverley* also serves as a critique of Romanticism. In Mayhead's opinion, the novel can be viewed as a sermon on the danger of being overly influenced by Romanticism. The title character is depicted as a man whose impressionable nature is largely a result of his Romantic predilections, such as a distaste for classical learning and a desire for amusement, which culminates in his support of the Stuart rebellion. However, Mayhead notes, Scott is not unsympathetic toward the Romantic attitudes of his hero, and the ambiguity possibly reflects Scott's own curious yet suspicious embrace of the Romantic movement. Mayhead is the author of *Understanding Literature* and *Walter Scott*, the book from which this selection is excerpted.

I offer no set definition of Romanticism, but we may agree that Scott shares certain fairly conspicuous characteristics with other major writers thought of as belonging to the movement. There is, for instance, his liking for wild scenery . . . , which links him with Wordsworth, Coleridge, Shelley, and the Byron of *Childe Harold.* Then his predilection for the supernatural, or sometimes just strong hints of the supernatural, connects him with the best-selling Romanticism of the so-called Tales of Terror, those precursors of the modern thriller, the [Gothic] novels of Mrs. [Anne] Radcliffe above all. In *Waverley* this element appears in Fergus Mac-Ivor's visions of the 'Bodach Glas', a traditional family spectre. Also related to the Tales of Terror, and to much of Byron, is a type of male character who may be roughly described as the 'hero-villain': a type in whom the proportion of good to evil, fair to threatening, varies from one specific example to another, but who always seems either to live under a curse or to be driven by an alarming obsessive energy, or both. Though other Scott novels contain clearer instances of the type (some, indeed, are excessively clear), Fergus Mac-Ivor is to some extent a subtle variant. Finally in this rough conspectus there is that attachment to the rural, the homespun, the traditional, which Scott shares with both Wordsworth and the Coleridge of *The Rime of the Ancient Mariner.*

DIFFERENT THAN OTHER ROMANTICS

But there is one thing Scott, in his imaginative work as distinct from his letters and *Journal,* does *not* have in common with most of the great Romantic figures: their concern with overtly *personal* emotion. He is not his own hero, as Wordsworth and Shelley, in very different ways, are respectively the heroes of *The Prelude* and the *Ode to the West Wind.* Of course all the Romantics wrote a deal of poetry that is far less self-directed, but it will hardly be denied that a preoccupation with emotion intensely personal to the author is a striking characteristic of the movement. Yet Scott, seemingly one of Romanticism's leading figures and certainly a most influential one, is quite without it.

This would suggest that in a major respect he is set apart from Romanticism in general. Indeed, it is tempting to join some modern enthusiasts in asserting that he is fundamentally anti-Romantic, explaining away most of the shared characteristics I have noted (though not the interest in the traditional) by the argument that he had to include such things to win a large popular audience. Yet to rush without large qualification to so extreme a view does not aid understanding of so complex a make-up as his. He was undoubtedly well aware of his audience, for he wanted to make money, but the prevalence of evidently Romantic elements in his work is too striking to be written off in all its manifestations merely as concession to popular taste. As for his being positively anti-Romantic, there is no major figure of the movement, with the possible exception of Shelley, of whom this could not be said, if one wished, with regard to some of his work—which is a good reason for only using the term 'Romantic' broadly, without aiming for definition.

Instead of trying to see Scott as a crusader against Romanticism, then, let us consider the Romantic in *Waverley*, with two questions kept particularly in mind. Firstly, if Scott often appears to be anti-Romantic, to what extent and in what sense is it really true? Secondly, if we discount the argument of concession to popular taste, do the evidently Romantic things in the book have a definite function?

Edward Waverley's Romantic Disposition

There certainly is warrant for supposing this novel to be a kind of fictional sermon against Romanticism as an influence upon the individual life. Here the account in the early chapters of Edward Waverley's boyhood and his attitude towards learning has an evident importance, for Scott will later wish us to understand that the adult Waverley is what his education has made him. Take this, from Chapter 3:

> His powers of apprehension were so uncommonly quick as almost to resemble intuition, and the chief care of his preceptor was to prevent him, as a sportsman would phrase it, from overrunning his game—that is, from acquiring his knowledge in a slight, flimsy, and inadequate manner. And here the instructor had to combat another propensity too often united with brilliancy of fancy and vivacity of talent—that indolence, namely, of disposition, which can only be stirred by some strong motive of gratification, and which renounces study as soon as curiosity is gratified, the pleasure of conquering the first difficulties exhausted, and the novelty of pursuit is at an end. Edward would throw himself with spirit upon any classical author of which his preceptor proposed the perusal, make himself master of the style so far as to understand the story, and, if that pleased or interested him, he finished the volume. But it was in vain to attempt fixing his attention on critical distinctions of philology, upon the difference of idiom, the beauty of felicitous expression, or the artificial combinations of syntax. 'I can read and understand a Latin author,' said young Edward, with the self-confidence and rash reasoning of fifteen, 'and Scaliger or Bentley could not do much more.' Alas! while he was thus permitted to read only for the gratification of his amusement, he foresaw not that he was losing for ever the opportunity of acquiring habits of firm and assiduous application, of gaining the art of controlling, directing, and concentrating the powers of his mind for earnest investigation—an art far more essential than even

that intimate acquaintance with classical learning which is
the primary object of study.   (14)

Only readers approaching the book as mainly an historical
chronicle could agree with those who think such passages
tiresomely unnecessary. As will be seen later, Scott does
have an interest in the '45,[1] which we can, in a special sense,
call 'historical'; but in this book he is neither a painstaking
assembler of documentation nor a purveyor of the modern
historical bestseller's 'background colour'. One of his cardi-
nal preoccupations, indeed, is more properly described as
psychological: a preoccupation with the seductive appeal of
the Stuart cause for such a person as Waverley, whose impressionable nature is so much the product of early habits.
Yet, despite his weaknesses, Waverley cannot be seen as con-
demned with a harsh austerity in the passage just quoted.
Scott may shake his head at opportunities lost, he may regret
that Waverley was intellectually so undisciplined, but there
is more than a touch of sympathy for the teenager who dis-
regards 'critical distinctions of philology' and 'the artifical
combinations of syntax' in favour of the straight question
'Does the book I am reading interest me or not?' If Scott is
asking us to look at him critically, he is not inviting us to be
too gravely censorious.

Chapter 4, which continues the story of Waverley's formation, introduces us to his ardently romantic predilections.
(The word 'romantic' will be printed without a capital when
its reference is to individual disposition, while the form 'Romantic' will be used for references specifically literary or
artistic.) Not only does reading play acutely upon his sensibility; he can be roused by conjuring up visions of stirring,
picturesque, or pathetic events in his own family's past.
Here, for instance, we find him day-dreaming about the dramatic return home of Wilibert of Waverley:

> In the corner of the large and sombre library, with no other
> light than was afforded by the decaying brands on its pon-
> derous and ample hearth, he would exercise for hours that
> internal sorcery by which past or imaginary events are pre-
> sented in action, as it were, to the eye of the muser. Then
> arose in long and fair array the splendour of the bridal feast
> at Waverley Castle; the tall and emaciated form of its real
> lord, as he stood in his pilgrim's weeds, an unnoticed specta-

1. Jacobites were supporters of James II and the direct Stuart line after the English
Revolution of 1688, when William and Mary took the throne. The Jacobites held unsuccessful uprisings in 1715 and 1745 to restore the Stuarts to the throne.

> tor of the festivities of his supposed heir and intended bride;
> the electrical shock occasioned by the discovery; the spring-
> ing of the vassals to arms; the astonishment of the bride-
> groom; the terror and confusion of the bride; the agony with
> which Wilibert observed that her heart as well as consent
> was in these nuptials; the air of dignity, yet of deep feeling,
> with which he flung down the half-drawn sword, and turned
> away for ever from the house of his ancestors.   (21)

That passage is of special interest. For besides being part of
the laying bare of Waverley's romantic disposition, the disposition that will make him impulsively pledge himself to
Prince Charles Edward, it is also extremely personal to the
author, Walter Scott.

WAVERLEY IS NOT SCOTT

Now that may seem to contradict what I said about the absence in Scott of the overtly personal. Actually there is no
contradiction. Edward Waverley is not the novelist in dis-
guise. Here, as elsewhere in his work, Scott is not his own
hero. But in the character of Waverley, and in the whole
working-out of the book, he is investigating problems and
tensions which were acutely his, dramatizing them through
a fictional hero and the circumstances in which he is placed
rather than giving them directly personal expression. Instead of saying 'I, Walter Scott, have a basically romantic disposition, and often feel uncomfortable about it, little as I care
to give it up', he explores the matter in terms of a character
very different from himself. At least, Waverley is quite different from Scott the man as regards weaker personality
traits, though the latter's adventures in business and prop-
erty, pursued with rash exuberance, might strike us, however unromantic they sound in themselves, as expressing a
spirit not wholly unlike that which leads his hero into join-
ing an armed rebellion.

But that is to stray into biography, intriguing as it is. What
most relevantly emerges from our passage is something
which links up with one side of Scott as a *novelist;* for he is
here analysing, in terms of the fictitious Edward Waverley,
that predilection for evoking the past for its own picturesque
sake which was later to produce what I called in the first
chapter the 'historical fantasias'. The imagined return of
Wilibert of Waverley is exactly the kind of event upon which
the big 'scenes' of those novels are often based. Yet here, in
his very first novel, Scott is looking at that predilection for

history embodied in the obviously colourful and dramatic with definitely critical eyes. He does not castigate Waverley so as to alienate the reader's sympathy, but his critical posi-

SCOTT'S REALISTIC CHARACTERS

Eino Railo, the author of The Haunted Castle: A Study of the Elements of English Romanticism, *asserts that Sir Walter Scott is a Romantic writer whose stories are also highly realistic. Rather than rely on the larger than life characters common to early Romantic novels, Scott creates believable individuals.*

Full-blooded a romanticist as was Scott, he was notwithstanding a rarely sane and sharp-eyed dweller in realities. In his romances we find a series of characters depicted with so much truth to nature, down to the finest turns of speech, that their creation must have demanded much observation and an unusual memory. His Scotch hags, beggars, Highlanders, farmers and officials, are no products of imagination, but persons who had come within the range of his own experiences; this side of his work provides one of the first examples of the realistic treatment of scenes from the life of the people. Scott's "realism" merits the attribute much better than the naturalism of the picaresque novels, which is, in reality, based on those romantic tales of artful rascals which form one of the elements of folk-lore. A special depth and a touch of modernity is given to Scott's descriptions of popular life by the strong sympathy, upborne by a wise humour, with which he regards his characters, a sympathy which reveals to us a worthy soul beneath rags or an otherwise modest exterior. This feeling for reality, this sympathy and love for his people, is extended to the heroines, and as his own manly, chivalrous character inclined him to dreams of ideal young womanhood, the outcome of these two influences was a type of maiden no longer to be classed with Mrs. Radcliffe's Emilys and Julias, with the damsels of castles or the dark-curled beauties of tradition, but a vigorous, healthy, natural Scotch girl of the type of Jeanie Deans in *The Heart of Midlothian.* . . .

In such characters Scott was, in my view, at his highest as an artist, raising an originally bloodless and conventionally romantic lay-figure to a stage of individuality upon which Dickens was later to base his own characters. Thus through Scott, the young heroine becomes a living being, treading paths totally dissimilar to those trodden by her sister, the ethereal idealist of Southey and Shelley.

Eino Railo, *The Haunted Castle: A Study of the Elements of English Romanticism.* New York: Humanities Press, 1964.

tion is clear from the heading of Chapter 4: 'Castle-Building'. And consider, moreover, the words which end the chapter:

> Through these scenes it was that Edward loved to 'chew the cud of sweet and bitter fancy', and, like a child among his toys, culled and arranged, from the splendid yet useless imagery and emblems with which his imagination was stored, visions as brilliant and as fading as those of an evening sky. The effect of this indulgence upon his temper and character will appear in the next chapter.   (22)

The romantic propensity is there seen as both childish and futile, as the manifestation of a prolonged and potentially damaging immaturity.

ROMANTIC AND ANTI-ROMANTIC

Scott's attitude has more to it than that judgement alone, however, for the critically observed propensity, even at this stage of his career, is a very real part of the author's make-up. To look at something critically is not to say that in all its manifestations one altogether despises it. The very fact that so much of Scott's later, if far less interesting, work drew largely upon the 'Castle-Building' vein proves that he did not write it off. What seems to have happened is that he came to exploit the vein more or less uncritically. It was popular, it paid dividends. To that extent those who argue that he was guided by the market in his use of Romantic material are justified. But they are not right in supposing that he was ever merely cynical in using it, or that in a book like *Waverley* it figures as a sop to popular taste.

The position may be suggested as follows: *Waverley* is the work of a writer deeply attracted by the wild, the picturesque, the stirring, yet who is at the same time acutely suspicious of their charms; a man who believes that the individual unduly swayed by them will at best be incomplete and at worst court sheer disaster. Scott is both Romantic *and* anti-Romantic. He is at once a Romantic at heart, and a vigilant critic of his own Romanticism.

A Cautious Acceptance of Romanticism in Austen's *Persuasion*

June Dwyer

In her novel *Persuasion*—her last complete work—
Jane Austen develops characters who have more Romantic qualities than those in her earlier books.
However, notes June Dwyer, Austen remains a critic
of the most excessive qualities of romanticism. The
two main characters in the novel—Anne Elliott and
Captain Frederick Wentworth—display certain Romantic characteristics, such as a belief in the constancy of love and delight in nature, that Austen
finds praiseworthy. However, Austen is critical of the
more excessive qualities displayed by Captain Benwick and Louisa Musgrove, associating those characters with self-indulgent and childish behavior.
Dwyer is the chair of the English department at
Manhattan College in Riverdale, New York.

[Jane Austen's] *Persuasion* is a novel about constancy, about
the persistence of love when hope is gone. Instead of the
sense of possibility that marked the Dashwood girls'
prospects in *Sense and Sensibility, Persuasion* dwells on the
unique quality of one particular match and the inappropri-
ateness of any other in comparison to it. At nineteen, Anne
Elliot is forced to refuse an offer of marriage from a young
sailor, Frederick Wentworth, whose initial lack of fortune
makes him an objectionable choice to her cold, aristocratic
family. At twenty-seven she still loves him, and because of
her continuing attachment she has refused another offer of
marriage from the rich and good-hearted Charles Musgrove.
She is prepared to turn down a third proposal as well, this
one from her wealthy and superficially charming cousin,
William Elliot. Instead of working toward a proper match as

Austen's novels usually do, *Persuasion* begins after a proper match has been thwarted. In this story Austen rethinks Elinor Dashwood's sage observation in *Sense and Sensibility* that no one's happiness depends entirely on one particular person. Anne Elliot's happiness does. After once having been in love with Frederick Wentworth, she has no interest in anyone else. . . .

PATIENCE AND PASSIVITY

The word *persuasion* is used in two senses in the novel—both in the active sense of convincing and in the more passive sense of holding an opinion. Austen's appreciation that people cannot totally control events, that Providence *will* take a hand, makes her favor the second kind of persuasion. She sees to it that those characters who are overly resolute in their actions or overly insistent in their opinions precipitate unwelcome events. Louisa Musgrove's determination to jump off the wall at Lyme leads to her serious physical injury. And the Elliots' insistence that Anne refuse Frederick Wentworth leads to her emotional injury.

Clearly, Austen does not champion passivity in *Persuasion*, but she does favor strength of opinion that is tempered by a willingness to acquiesce and to wait. In one of the book's minor incidents, Charles Hayter, who wishes to marry Henrietta Musgrove, thinks himself in danger of being supplanted by Captain Wentworth. After a short struggle, he appears to quit the field, and although the others are mystified, Anne understands that "Charles Hayter was wise." His withdrawal causes Henrietta to seek him out and declare her affection for him. Charles has been neither passive nor overly assertive; he struggles briefly before seeming to withdraw his bid. Like Anne, who admires his behavior, he knows both how to assert himself and how to wait.

Although Anne's and Charles Hayter's behavior is the preferred course of action in Austen's mind, she is honest enough to demonstrate that it carries no guarantee of success. Luckily for Charles, his withdrawal brings about an immediate reaction, but Anne must wait eight years to become reacquainted with Frederick Wentworth, and then it is purely by chance. Because of the unpredictable role that fortune plays in life, Austen favors neither overly rational insistence nor overly Romantic assertiveness. Both stances presuppose a control over events that does not exist in the world of *Persuasion*.

OVERINDULGENT ROMANTICISM IS CRITICIZED

Although Austen moves closer in *Persuasion* to an appreciation of some of the tenets of Romanticism, she is still leery of
its tendency toward self-indulgence. She willingly pictures
Anne's Romantic reaction to the wildness of Lyme—her
glow from the sea air and her heartfelt joy in the beauty of
the scenery. But she will not condone the Romantic excesses
of Captain Benwick, whose wretchedness over the death of
his fiancée Fanny Harville is fed by a steady diet of Byron's
poetry. Indeed, Anne counsels him to read prose as a cor-
rective, suggesting that the rational work of the best English
moralists will calm his turmoil. In the end, Benwick's Romantic devotion proves less sincere and enduring than
Anne's more reserved suffering. With shocking alacrity he
forgets both his grief and his lost love, proposing marriage to
the recuperating Louisa Musgrove. She is a fine-hearted girl
but a most unusual choice for a suffering Romantic.

The most excessive elements of Romanticism appeal least
to Austen, and she makes a point of associating them with
self-indulgence and childishness. Louisa Musgrove's exu-
berant leap off the Cobb at Lyme recalls the fall of Anne's
frolicking young nephew at the beginning of the story. After
each accident it is Anne who capably takes over, in sharp
contrast to the other women on the scene who faint and fret.
There is no childishness on her part but rather an adult effort to bring order and control to the situation. In each case,
Captain Wentworth is her second, willing to be of assistance
and admiring of her sweet and steady usefulness.

Of course Anne, too, has taken a kind of fall—she has
fallen in love and suffered from it. But hers is not a childish
or self-indulgent fall. Her devotion is deep and persistent,
kept painfully inside and shared with no one. Over and over,
Anne's efforts to master her emotions are stressed as she re-
news her acquaintance with Captain Wentworth. In Anne
the reader sees an openness to Romantic feeling but never
an indulgence of herself in it.

TYPES OF FAMILIES

Openness is a new virtue for Austen and a necessary one to
the society that she pictures in *Persuasion*. The landed gentry, personified in Anne's father Sir Walter Elliot, has become ossified—spendthrift, isolated, and self-absorbed. Sir
Walter's preoccupation with the past and with the preserva-

tion of appearances, along with his distaste for the new men of the navy who are elevated to wealth and prominence because of their competence, indicates his own want of substance. He has nothing to offer but "heartless elegance" and the empty shell of his snobbery.

Because she is not like her father and her sisters, Anne is routinely excluded by them and treated little better than a servant. She finds in Captain Wentworth and his friends a welcome change—a brotherly, open, friendly society. Shining through their conversation, their kindness, and their good sense is a worthiness suggesting that they are the new aristocracy. Anne herself views the Crofts, who have rented the Elliot estate, as more appropriate occupants for that aristocratic seat than her own family. She thinks to herself, "they were gone who deserved not to stay ... Kellynch-hall had passed into better hands."

Jane Austen

The insistence on the brotherliness and the friendliness of the navy families suggests that, as well as their being the new aristocracy, they are also the new family. Experience rather than birth binds them together, and Anne, all but ostracized from her own family, looks longingly to them for companionship. Their ready appreciation of her merits and their willing welcome add to the strength of the bond. In her previous novels, Austen had insisted that rank is not enough, that the landed gentry must also have character in order to merit respect. But only in *Persuasion* does she offer an alternative to the landed gentry. Frederick Wentworth does not come from a gentleman's family the way that all of Austen's other heroes do; instead he is a natural gentleman. In her abandonment of the hero who is the son or heir of an aristocratic family, Austen in yet another way is stepping into the camp of the Romantics.

But Austen is not totally embracing democratic idealism. Anne is still a member of the landed gentry and her marriage to Captain Wentworth will fuse the best of two classes of English society. In contrast, her cousin William Elliot's first marriage brought together two of the most objectionable elements of English society. Overly eager to regain wealth that his family had lost, the greedy and heartless Elliot married a tradesman's daughter for her money and then mistreated her. Unlike Anne, the young woman lacked the discernment to suspect her suitor's motives. The result of the union was misery and an early death for the wife and further social climbing for the widowed husband. The newly wealthy William Elliot then proceeds to use his breeding—his good manners and agreeable conversation—as a tool to achieve even greater aristocratic status in the courting of his cousin.

ROMANTIC ALTERATIONS

Anne realizes that were there no Captain Wentworth, she might well have been prevailed upon to accept her cousin's offer of marriage. Once she knows his true character, this thought chills her and conveys to the reader Austen's fears that the noble elements of the English aristocracy (embodied in Anne) were threatened through such inbreeding. In her earlier draft of what became chapters 22 and 23 of *Persuasion*, Austen has Captain Wentworth actually confront Anne (at his brother-in-law Admiral Croft's behest) to ascertain whether she is engaged to William Elliot. Unaware of Captain Wentworth's attachment to Anne, the admiral wishes only to know if he should volunteer to give up his lease on Kellynch-hall so that a new generation of Elliots might dwell there. The situation provides Anne with an opportunity to deny the rumor of her engagement to her cousin and gives Wentworth an opportunity to declare his love for her.

The episode is neither awkwardly conceived nor executed; however, as written, it underlines Austen's social preoccupation with the moribund state of the aristocracy. The reader is asked to envision Kellynch-hall, symbol of the soulless landed gentry, losing the revivifying presence of its new tenant, Admiral Croft. Instead Anne Elliot, its last warmhearted and right-living member, will spend what is sure to be an unhappy married life there, yoked to her scheming cousin, William. Fortunately, this vision does not become a reality, for Anne is able to resist marrying Mr. Elliot. As long as Captain Wentworth's open and vital presence remains on the scene, her cousin's calculating charm can never win her.

When Austen revised *Persuasion's* twenty-third chapter,

she changed its focus from the social to the personal, and in doing so, she made it a document of the Romantic era. In place of the dutiful inquiry from Frederick Wentworth about Anne's marriage plans and their effect on the Admiral's living arrangements, the rewritten chapter shows him eagerly eavesdropping on a conversation between her and Captain Harville. Their discussion concerns ideas and emotions rather than practical particulars; the topic is not tenancy but constancy.

LOVE AND CONSTANCY

Captain Harville maintains that men's feelings are stronger and more persistent than women's, while Anne counters that women's feelings are deeper and more tender. She argues that in staying quietly confined at home, women are more often prey to their feelings while men, who go out into the world, soon are entangled in activities that eclipse their tender emotions. When Captain Harville cites the frequent theme of the fickle woman in literature, Anne replies, "Men have had every advantage of us in telling their own story. Education has been theirs in so much higher a degree; the pen has been in their hands. I will not allow books to prove anything."

The emotionally charged argument continues with each party understanding but not persuading the other. This overheard exchange precipitates Frederick Wentworth's proposal in a letter that he writes on the spot and wordlessly delivers to Anne as he leaves the house. Although he does not agree with her, he has been greatly moved by her eloquence about women's constancy and especially by the note of experience in her voice when she states that women, unlike men, love when hope is gone.

Significantly, Anne's exchange with Captain Harville is a conversation between equals and not a one-sided persuasion, a judgment handed down by a superior to his inferior. Indeed, Captain Harville's responsiveness to Anne's arguments indicates in yet another way the democratic openness of the navy men and their way of life. Having heard the discussion and been moved to propose to Anne again, Captain Wentworth also demonstrates that there is a democratic level of persuasion where one listens to both sides and then independently makes a decision.

The direct inquiry into whether Anne is to marry her cousin that spurred Captain Wentworth's proposal in the original chapter 23 has disappeared from the revised version. In the reworked chapter Anne, rather than refuting a rumor, explains her beliefs and exposes her feelings. Wentworth's response is immediate and decidedly Romantic. Unable to wait until he can be alone with her, he pours out his intimate feelings in a letter. Using the written word not to complain of woman's fickleness but to persuade Anne of his own constant love, Wentworth can be seen as a new kind of writer. He is beginning a new book, a book about Romantic love and marriage, a book that will supersede Sir Walter Elliot's tired old tome on the Baronetage that we see him reading as the novel opens. Unlike the Baronetage, that recorded so many loveless unions from the past, this new volume has a different content altogether. It is not a history of Wentworth's family; it is a history of his feelings. The revised chapter 23 does not present Captain Wentworth's marriage to Anne as a way of breathing new life into the aristocracy, but instead it ushers the novel's characters and its readers into the Romantic era. Here feeling is more important than tradition, and an individual may embark upon a new way of life.

A Different Austen Novel

Persuasion is Jane Austen's most intriguing novel not only because it is her last complete narrative, but also because it departs most radically from her usual variations on the theme of finding a mate. As with her other fiction, the subject of *Persuasion* is courting. However, its picture of the Crofts' happy marriage and of Anne's nearly thwarted union with Captain Wentworth may indicate that Austen had begun moving, albeit slowly, into other realms. Clearly, she had at least begun to consider relegating happy marriage to a subplot and bringing unrequited love to center stage. Had Austen lived even one more decade, her readers may well have witnessed her writing about women who steadfastly refused to marry or who found themselves married to the wrong man. She may quite easily have stepped into the territory that was soon to be held by the Brontës and George Eliot.

Despite the suggestion of harsher realities rumbling beneath the surface, in the end, *Persuasion* maintains Austen's faith in the desirability of love and marriage more strongly than ever. It seems clear that at forty the author would still have welcomed an appropriate marriage for herself, just as she welcomed one for the "older" Anne Elliot. The possibility of late marriage had been on Austen's mind for several years. In her previous novel, *Emma*, she portrayed the happy union of her heroine's thirty-five year old governess Anna Taylor to an attractive widower. Although this particular marriage is based on sincere affection, it is also a logical and practical step for both parties.

Anne Elliot's marriage to Frederick Wentworth is, in contrast, a considerably more romantic union. She has known no other men, and he, no other women. The singularity of their match, odd as it may initially seem, also suggests that Austen was moving away from happy marriages and happy endings in her novels. The very idea that there could have been no one for Anne but Captain Wentworth and that she very nearly missed marrying him, suggests that the author had begun to see a thin line between happiness and deep sadness. The more rational world of her earlier novels where a woman looked around and saw many prospects for a good life has been, if not transformed, at least modified. *Persuasion's* happy ending is not like Austen's other happy endings. Events could not have simply turned out differently—they could have turned out tragically.

Mary Shelley: *Frankenstein*

Muriel Spark

In this essay, Muriel Spark focuses on the subtitle of Mary Shelley's novel *Frankenstein or the Modern Prometheus*. Mary Shelley reflects on the meaning of the Prometheus myth. In Greek mythology, Prometheus was a Titan who helped create life but was punished by Zeus for going against the god's wish and giving humans the valuable gift of fire. Two important elements link Victor Frankenstein and his monster to Prometheus. Frankenstein uses fire—or, rather, its modern equivalent electricity—to animate his monster. Frankenstein also rebels against God by creating life, thus usurping the divine role. In the original myth, Prometheus' punishment involved being chained to a rock. Shelley adds movement to the Prometheus story by making pursuits a central theme of *Frankenstein*—first, the monster pursues his creator, Frankenstein, and then Frankenstein chases his creation in response to the monster's murder of Frankenstein's bride. During the pursuits, the reader sees how the emotional and rational aspects of Frankenstein are in conflict. That conflict is Romantic in theme and also mirrors Mary Shelley's own struggle between Romantic and rationalist ideals. Mary Shelley resolves this conflict by having her characters undergo psychological compensation, a process akin to repentance, and having the rational monster repent and die in an overly Romantic manner. Spark is a novelist, biographer, and poet whose works include books on Mary Shelley and the Brontës.

Excerpted from Muriel Spark, *Mary Shelley*. Copyright © 1987 Copyright Administration Ltd. Reprinted with permission from David Higham Associates.

Perhaps because *Frankenstein* was born of ideas not fully re-
alised by its author but through the dream-like vision she
had described,[1] there are several ways in which it can be
considered; this variety of interpretative levels is part of its
artistic validity.

{There are two central figures—or rather two in one, for
Frankenstein and his significantly unnamed Monster are
bound together by the nature of their relationship. Frankenstein's plight resides in the Monster, and the Monster's in
Frankenstein} That this fact has received wide, if unwitting,
recognition is apparent from the common mistake of nam-
ing the Monster "Frankenstein" and emanates from the first
principle of the story, that Frankenstein is perpetuated in the
Monster. Several implicit themes show these characters as
both complementary and antithetical beings.

The most obvious theme is that suggested by the title,
Frankenstein—Or, The Modern Prometheus. (That casual, alternative *Or* is worth noting, for though at first Frankenstein
is himself the Prometheus, the vital fire-endowing protago-
nist, the Monster, as soon as he is created, takes on the role.
His solitary plight—". . . but am I not alone, miserably
alone?" he cries—and more especially his revolt against his
creator establish his Promethean features. So, the title im-
plies, the Monster is an alternative Frankenstein.)

The humanist symbol of Prometheus was one that occupied [Percy Bysshe] Shelley in many forms beside that of his
Prometheus Unbound, and Shelley's influence on Mary had
gained time to give figurative shape to [her father, William]
Godwin's view of mankind's situation. It is curious that Shelley should have written in his Preface to *Frankenstein:*

> The opinions which naturally spring from the character and
> situation of the hero are by no means to be conceived as ex-
> isting always in my [that is, Mary's] own conviction; nor is
> any inference justly to be drawn from the following pages as
> prejudicing any philosophical doctrine of whatever kind.

Curious, because one cannot help inferring a philosophical
attitude; but not so curious when we remember Shelley's refusal to admit the didactic element in his own poetry.

Less curious, however, is the epigraph to the book (original edition):

1. *Frankenstein* was inspired by a nightmare Mary had in the summer of 1816, when
she and Percy Shelley lived in Switzerland and spent much of their time visiting Lord
Byron and reading ghost stories.

Did I request thee, Maker, from my clay
To mould me man? Did I solicit thee
From darkness to promote me?

Paradise Lost

The motif of revolt against divine oppression, and indeed, against the concept of a benevolent deity, which is prominent in much of Shelley's thought, underlines the "Modern Prometheus" theme of *Frankenstein.* "You accuse me of murder," the Monster reproaches his maker, "and yet you would, with a satisfied conscience, destroy your own creature"—not the least of *Frankenstein's* echoes from Shelley.

The Prometheus myth is one of action but not of movement; that is, the main activity of the original story is located around the tortured Prometheus himself, chained to one spot. A novel, however, demands a certain range of activity, and in *Frankenstein* the action is released from its original compression by a secondary theme—that of pursuit, influenced most probably by Godwin's *Caleb Williams*. It is this theme that endows the novel, not only with movement, but with a pattern, easily discernible because it is a simple one.

It begins at Chapter V with the creation of the Monster who becomes, within the first two pages, Frankenstein's pursuer. He is removed for a time from the vicinity of his quarry, but continues to stalk the regions of Frankenstein's imagination, until it is discovered that he has been actually prosecuting his role through the murder of Frankenstein's young brother, William. Frankenstein is then hounded from his homeland to the remote reaches of the Orkney Islands where he is to propitiate his tormentor by creating a Monster-bride for him.

If we can visualise this pattern of pursuit as a sort of figure-of-eight macaberesque—executed by two partners moving with the virtuosity of skilled ice-skaters—we may see how the pattern takes shape in a movement of advance and retreat. Both partners are moving in opposite directions, yet one follows the other. At the crossing of the figure eight they all but collide. Such a crossing occurs when Frankenstein faces his Monster alone in the mountains, and another, when Frankenstein makes his critical decision to destroy his nearly completed female Monster. Once these crises are passed, however, we find Frankenstein and the Monster moving apparently away from each other, but still prosecuting the course of their pattern. It is not until Frankenstein, on his bridal night, finds his wife murdered by the Monster that the roles are reversed. Frankenstein (to keep our image) increases his speed of execution, and the Monster slows down; now, at Chapter XXIV, Frankenstein becomes the pursuer, the Monster, the pursued.

Thenceforward, this theme becomes the central focus of the story. Motives have already been established, and we are induced to forget them, since hunter and hunted alike find a mounting exhilaration in the chase across frozen Arctic wastes, until it becomes the sole *raison d'être* of both. Frankenstein is urged in his pursuit, and in fact sustained, by the Monster:

> Sometimes, indeed, he left marks in writing on the barks of the trees, or cut in stone, that guided me and instigated my fury. (. . .) "You will find near this place, if you follow not too tardily, a dead hare; eat and be refreshed. Come on, my enemy."

And one of the most memorable passages in the book occurs where the Monster again instructs his creator:

> "Wrap yourself in furs and provide food; for we shall soon enter upon a journey where your sufferings will satisfy my everlasting hatred."

I find that "wrap yourself in furs" very satisfying; as I do Frankenstein's rationalisation of his own fanatical relish in the chase; he swears:

> to pursue the dæmon who caused this misery until he or I shall perish in mortal conflict. For this purpose I will preserve my life.

until he comes to conceive himself divinely appointed to the task, his purpose "assigned . . . by Heaven."

The whole ironic turn of events is, I think, a stroke of genius. Mary's treatment of this theme alone elevates her book above *Caleb Williams* and other novels which deal with the straight-forward hunter-and-hunted theme. By these means the figures retain their poise to the very end. No collision occurs, and the pattern is completed only by Frankenstein's natural death and the representation of the Monster hanging over him in grief. They merge one into the other, entwined in final submission.

The pattern of pursuit is the framework of the novel, a theme in itself which encloses a further theme; there, Frankenstein's relationship to the Monster expresses itself in the paradox of identity and conflict—an anticipation of the Jekyll-and-Hyde theme—from which certain symbolic situations emerge.

Frankenstein himself states:

> I considered the being whom I had cast among mankind (. . .)
> nearly in the light of my own vampire, my own spirit let loose
> from the grave, and forced to destroy all that was dear to me.

We may visualise Frankenstein's doppelgänger or Monster firstly as representing reason in isolation, since he is the creature of an obsessional rational effort. The manifest change in Frankenstein's nature after the creation of the Monster can be explained by the part-separation of his intellect from his other integral properties. He becomes a sort of Hamlet figure, indecisive and remorseful too late. He decides to destroy the Monster, but is persuaded to pity him—he decides to make a female Monster, but fails at the last moment—he receives the Monster's threat of revenge and does nothing: "Why had I not followed him, and closed with him in mortal strife? But I had suffered him to depart," Frankenstein muses bitterly when the damage has been done. And he admits,

> through the whole period during which I was the slave of my
> creature, I allowed myself to be governed by the impulses of
> the moment.

After the Monster's "birth," then, Frankenstein is a disintegrated being—an embodiment of emotion and also of imagination minus intellect. When, in his final reflections, Frankenstein realises that it was not always so, and exclaims,

> My imagination was vivid, yet my powers of analysis and application were intense; by the union of these qualities I conceived the idea and executed the creation of a man.

he reminds us of those eighteenth-century geniuses (the story of Frankenstein is set in that century) whose too-perfect balance of imaginative and rational faculties did in fact so often disintegrate and ultimately destroy them.

Generally speaking, therefore, it is the emotional and the intellectual that conflict in the form of Frankenstein and his Monster. The culminating emotional frustration by the intellect is reached in the murder of Frankenstein's bride by the Monster. Thereafter, Frankenstein's hysterical pursuit of his fleeting reason completes the story of his madness—a condition perceived in the tale only by the Genevan magistrate, who, when Frankenstein demands of him the Monster's arrest, "endeavoured," says Frankenstein, "to soothe me as a nurse does a child."

Richard Church recognised a parallel in Mary Shelley's

life when he discussed the murder of Frankenstein's brother, William. "At the time that she was writing this book," Mr. Church remarks, "the baby William was in the tenderest and most intimate stage of dependent infancy. . . . It is almost inconceivable that Mary could allow herself to introduce a baby boy into her book; deliberately call him William, describe him in terms identical with those in which she portrays her own child in one of her letters—and then let Frankenstein's monster waylay this innocent in a woodland dell and murder him by strangling."

It *is* almost inconceivable; and Mr. Church described Mary's motives as a "miserable delight in self-torture." But another suggestion by Mr. Church might give a clue to this coincidence. The creature who murdered William "was a symbol of Mary's overtrained intellectual conscience." The conflict between the emotional and the intellectual Frankenstein was Mary Shelley's also. Her baby, William, we know was the child Mary loved more than any; and when she began to feel her intellect grow under her new task, she automatically identified the child with her threatened emotions.

But the symbolic ramifications of the Jekyll-and-Hyde theme reach further than Mary's own life. For so far as she, like others of her time, was beginning to work out her own philosophical mind, her *Frankenstein* expresses the prevalent frustrated situation and reaction to it; the dichotomous elements in the novel are those which were tormenting the ethos. As Frankenstein clashed with his Monster, so did fixed religious beliefs with science; so did imaginative and emotional substitutes for religion with scientific rationalism; so did the intuitive and lush passions of the new era with the dialectical, material and succinct passions of the eighteenth century.

And *Frankenstein* represents, also, that unresolvable aspect of the Romantic temperament which was very soon to be expressed in the quasi-cult of Doubt. Shelley, it is true, had approached these issues with a more emphatic voice, a more perfect heart; his ideas were beliefs, not doubts, and Mary adapted many of them to her novel. But *Frankenstein*, I think, bears the signature of a less positive way of thought which nevertheless held sway in a large number of intelligent minds. Shelley, for example, would see Frankenstein, in his role of creator, as the perpetrator of human misery and therefore an object of hatred. And, Mary added, he is the sufferer from human misery and therefore an object of pity. But, she also added, he is an amoral product of nature, on whom no responsibility can be attached, towards whom no passion can logically be entertained. It was probably with some insight into the deadlock at which such propositions arrived that Shelley wrote his equivocal Preface to *Frankenstein.*

Although these questions, typical of the Romantic outlook, form the moral spirit of her novel, Mary Shelley does not allow them to end in deadlock, but resolves them by introducing a process of psychological compensation, which also has a counterpart in history. Her intellectual image, the Monster, comes to ultimate repentance. But his repentance has not the rational flavour of Calvinism; for his resolve to perish by fire has all the ecstatic feeling of Revivalism:[2]

> I shall ascend my funeral pile triumphantly, and exult in the agony of the torturing flames.

The more rigid the logic, therefore, the more fervent the imaginative reaction.

---

2. Calvinism is a theological system founded by John Calvin in the late sixteenth century. Its key tenet is the doctrine of predestination, which states that God has already decided who will be saved and who will be damned. Revivalism, a term that first appeared in 1815, refers to breathing new life into stagnant religious movements.

The Plain-Speaking Intimacy of Hazlitt's Essays

Christopher Salvesen

William Hazlitt is a writer who was famed for his essays on his Romantic contemporaries and William Shakespeare. Christopher Salvesen argues that Hazlitt was the greatest essayist of the Romantic era. The key quality of Hazlitt's essays is his straightforward language. His efforts to write in a conversational tone give even the lengthiest essays an intimate quality. Salvesen's writings include *The Landscape of Memory: A Study of Wordsworth's Poetry*.

After [William] Wordsworth, Hazlitt draws more fully on the sense of the past than any other English Romantic. All the same, the prime quality of Hazlitt's imagination is an energetic delight in ideas and their working-out. Ideas have a life of their own; Hazlitt's great virtue is to make them personal without reducing their vitality. A nostalgic temperament combines with supremely incisive thinking. This is not a matter of contrast; Hazlitt works with ideas which he has made his own through years of rehearsal. He knows and loves the repetitions of the mind, "still occupied with something interesting, still recalling some old impression, still recurring to some difficult question and making progress in it, every step accompanied with a sense of power." ("On the Past and Future"). He *owns* his speculations no less than his particular memories. For example, at the end of "A Farewell to Essay-Writing" (1828) he recalls a time when he used to walk out in the evenings with [essayist and literary critic] Charles and Mary Lamb,

> to look at the Claude Lorraine skies over our heads, melting from azure into purple and gold, and to gather mushrooms, that sprung up at our feet, to throw into our hashed mutton at

supper. . . . It is in looking back to such scenes that I draw my best consolation for the future. Later impressions come and go, and serve to fill up the intervals; but these are my standing resource, my true classics.

And he continues, still sounding the note of regret inseparable from such memories: "If I have had few real pleasures or advantages, my ideas, from their sinewy texture, have been to me in the nature of realities; and if I should not be able to add to my stock, I can live by husbanding the interest." His ideas have become almost a physical part of him ("I have brooded over an idea till it has become a kind of substance in my brain").

For Hazlitt, ideas are emotions; often reflected on, they remain ideas, opinions deeply grounded, forcefully put; yet they also come across with the impact of feelings. This may remind us of what T.S. Eliot discovered in early seventeenth-century poetry, "a direct sensuous apprehension of thought or a recreation of thought into feeling." But in the essays not only are ideas emotions, but we feel how these ideas have *become* emotions, in the strictly Romantic mode of growing. And yet their immediate coming across in Hazlitt's prose is what counts; there is no "dissociation of sensibility." The gap is closed, thanks to another feeling Hazlitt imparts, that of ideas *still* developing, "every step accompanied with a sense of power"; more generally, it is due to his remarkable ability to make thought and feeling cohere in the total form of an essay. One of the pleasures of a Hazlitt essay is to feel the "sinewy texture" of ideas both intellectually and emotionally, to be aware of ideas in action and of Hazlitt "husbanding the interest" on them. . . .

HAZLITT'S STYLE

The Hazlitt essay is one of the great formal achievements of English Romanticism. The form derives from Hazlitt's presence therein; he creates an authentic mode of shaping experience. "I have turned for consolation to the past, gathering up fragments of my early recollections, and putting them into a form that might live." We need not overemphasize the word "form" here; but Hazlitt pursues form unequivocally. It is sometimes remarked that he is at his best in small-scale works; but small is a relative term, and the Hazlitt essay (running to 7,000–8,000 words) is, by any standards applicable to the form in general, immense. At the same time it should be granted that the true scale of the essay is intimate; it is a personal colloquial mode. The essay is particularly interesting in being essentially discursive while at the same time being one of the most musical of prose forms. Its changes of mood and style (see, for example, "On the Feeling of Immortality in Youth") trace a rhythmic pattern which can be felt whole by the reader. Hazlitt once called his essays "these voluntaries of composition": one way of thinking of them formally, though used with some self-disparagement. He talked in similar terms of [Samuel] Coleridge's Watchman and Friend pieces; "whoever will be at pains to examine them closely, will find them to be *voluntaries*, fugues, solemn capriccios, not set compositions with any *malice prepense* in them, or much practical meaning." (Hazlitt's criticism of Coleridge often has this "symbolist" touch. Of "Kubla Khan" he writes: "It is not a poem, but a musical composition"; and he characterizes Coleridge as "the man of all others . . . to write marginal notes without a text"—which sounds like an adumbration of his alignment in Symbolist tradition, or the matter of a poem by Wallace Stevens.) The formal pattern of a Hazlitt essay is really a question

William Hazlitt

of what Hazlitt had heard Coleridge propound, "the metaphysical distinction between the grace of form, and the grace that arises from motion."

Style—the manner in which Hazlitt gets on with his argument and brings forward his personality—further defines the structure. Hazlitt the stylist is characterized by the title of his last collection of essays—the Plain Speaker. He is a rhetorician, concerned with the different ways of using language and of combining them effectively. He is interested in the musical qualities of prose, in rhapsody and exclamatory flights. But what he aims at most often is plain-speaking— the frank expression of opinion in straightforward language. This, Hazlitt knows, is difficult. His ideal is a "pure conversational prose-style"; hard to achieve because the exact word must always be found—the approximations of actual talk will not do:

> There is a research in the choice of a plain, as well as of an ornamental or learned style; and, in fact, a great deal more. Among common English words, there may be ten expressing the same thing with different degrees of force and propriety, and only one that answers exactly with the idea we have in our minds. Each word in familiar use has a different set of associations and shades of meaning attached to it . . . it is in having the whole of these at our command, and in knowing which to choose . . . that the perfection of a pure conversational prose-style consists.

And Hazlitt adds: "But in writing a florid and artificial style, neither the same range of invention, nor the same quick sense of propriety—nothing but learning is required." Hazlitt admits to versions of the florid in his own prose; but he recognizes the problem of any style however simple—that, being the product of "research," the difficulty is to preserve plainness. A history of English style might be written by working out what at any given time was meant by "plain" speaking. It is a Shakespearean concern ("Honest plain words best pierce the ear of grief," after the euphuistic fun of *Love's Labour's Lost*). Hazlitt, a stylist with a taste for rhapsody, and a reverence for poetry, considered the problem deeply as it affected the prose writer.

> It has always appeared to me that the most perfect prose-style, the most powerful, the most dazzling, the most daring, that which went nearest to the verge of poetry, and yet never fell over, was Burke's. . . . It differs from poetry . . . like the chamois from the eagle: it climbs to an almost equal height, touches upon a cloud, overlooks a precipice, is picturesque, sublime—but all the while, instead of soaring through the air, it stands upon a rocky cliff, clambers up by abrupt and intricate ways, and browzes on the roughest bark, or crops the tender flower.

Hazlitt here allows himself a "poetic" but appropriate illustration of [political theorist, Edmund] Burke, metaphorical without being fanciful, a brisk feet-on-the-ground "flight" doing homage to Burke's prose by providing a useful reminder of it. He goes on: "The principle which guides his pen is truth, not beauty—not pleasure, but power." Hazlitt as an essayist was nothing like so constrained as Burke, who "had to treat of political questions, mixed modes, abstract ideas, and his fancy (or poetry, if you will) was ingrafted on these artificially." But Hazlitt as prose writer is always committed to saying what is true, clearly. He is marked off from the poet, however powerfully he brings his "fancy or poetry" into play. Throughout the essays, he is intent on arguing a point, demonstrating a theory, maintaining a belief, "the professed object of prose is to impart conviction." The intellectual activity involved allows little room for merely decorative imagery: "Every word should be a blow: every thought should instantly grapple with its fellow." This interlocking ideal, with the texture of thought and the momentum of discovery, informs the Hazlitt essay. In discussing [poet John] Milton he indicates clearly the connection between the meaning and music of language. He defends Milton from the charge that because his ideas "were in the highest degree musical" they were not also powerfully descriptive, especially in the main subjects of *Paradise Lost*, "the daring ambition and fierce passions of Satan" and "the paradisaical happiness, and the loss of it" (Hazlitt responds fully to these twin themes of Revolution and Regret). He fully recognizes the power of "the language of music" because of its immediacy. But that "force of style" which is "one of Milton's great excellences" contains other elements. Of the speeches and debates in Pandemonium he notes:

> There is a decided manly tone in the arguments and sentiments, an eloquent dogmatism, as if each person spoke from thorough conviction; an excellence which Milton probably borrowed from his spirit of partisanship. . . . That approximation to the severity of impassioned prose which has been made an objection to Milton's poetry, and which is chiefly to be met with in these bitter invectives, is one of its great excellences.

"The severity of impassioned prose," with its fusion of style and conviction, is a Hazlitt ideal. Milton's style is both "musical" and "manly"; Hazlitt, as prose writer and political partisan, naturally admires it. The essayist discovered his "answerable style" in a similar mixture of plain speaking and passion.

INFLUENCES ON HAZLITT

Milton's own prose style dissatisfied Hazlitt; it savored "too much of poetry . . . and of an imitation of the Latin." But for Hazlitt ideals of poetry and conversation do not necessarily conflict with regard to prose. He considered Leigh Hunt's prose writing had "the raciness, the sharpness, and sparkling effect of poetry"; if there was also some "relaxation and trifling . . . still the genuine master-spirit of the prose-writer is there; the tone of lively sensible conversation." Hazlitt's own prose certainly displays this; it also has affinities with Coleridge's development of [William] Cowper's poetry (which Hazlitt admired), the Conversation Poem. The movement from colloquial ease to impassioned meditation, Coleridge's special achievement, likewise informs the Hazlitt essay. Hazlitt of course usually begins with an abstract proposition, and he aims to pursue a course of reasoning—but through a range of mood, in controlled, plain-speaking intimacy.

Hazlitt often returns to the relation of writing and speaking. He cites the opinion of [radical politician] Horne Tooke, that "no one could write a good prose style, who was not accustomed to express himself *viva voce* [out loud], or to talk in company." To which Hazlitt responds:

> I certainly so far agree with the above theory as to conceive that no style is worth a farthing that is not calculated to be read out, or that is not allied to spirited conversation; but I at the same time think the process of modulation and inflection may be quite as complete, or more so, without the external enunciation; and that an author had better try the effect of his sentences on his stomach than on his ear. He may be deceived by the last, not by the first.

The ultimate test is an inward one, involving the whole physical being and yet all but silent. He repeats the idea in his essay "On the Conversation of Authors": "there is a method of trying periods on the ear, or weighing them with the scales of the breath, without any articulate sound." And he adds, quoting from his friend J.S. Knowles, "Authors, as they write, may be said to 'hear a sound so fine, there's nothing lives 'twixt it and silence.' Even musicians generally compose in their heads." Hazlitt recognizes that all imaginative language, if it does not aspire to the condition of music, at least approaches musical composition. But he concludes by remarking, "I agree that no style is good, that is not fit to be spoken or read aloud with effect. This holds true not only of emphasis and cadence, but also with regard to natural idiom and colloquial freedom. Sterne's was in this respect the best style that ever was written. You fancy that you hear the people talking." It is a rarer quality than you might think; but in Hazlitt's style too you hear the man talking, a clear energetic voice beautifully informed with common sense, with deep feeling, with conviction.

Critiquing the Movement

English
Romanticism

The Decline of English Romanticism

Derek Colville

The Romantic movement declined as some of the Romantics, particularly William Wordsworth and Thomas Carlyle, became increasingly conservative as they aged, explains Derek Colville in the following viewpoint. As he reaches middle age, William Wordsworth is no longer influenced by his earlier vision. Thomas Carlyle becomes a political propagandist who scorns democracy. In essence the radical idealism that marked the earlier works of these writers was replaced by Victorian moralism. Colville is the author of *The Teaching of Wordsworth* and *Victorian Poetry and the Romantic Religion*, the book from which this viewpoint was excerpted.

[Romanticism's] most remarkable feature is the swiftness of its decay. One does not need much imagination to suggest its causes in Victorian England: the obliteration of much of an agricultural economy, and its replacement by an industrial one, bringing the sudden growth of cities and the varied problems of mass production; the struggle for political influence by large sections of the population; colonial expansion and exploitation; the pace and lack of leisure in materialistic life; the inadequacy of the church, despite attempts to reform it; science, especially in the fear, which Darwin symbolized, that nature, far from being a link in a chain leading to God, was itself the final reality—and one due to the operations of chance in an indifferent universe. All that has since happened to many of these thorny Victorian problems is that they have developed a broader milieu and have become more pressing.

WORDSWORTH'S CONSERVATISM

Romantic decline is illustrated by almost all the writers I have mentioned who lived into middle age. A generally sympathetic critic of Wordsworth remarks of his development, ". . . for the most part after 1805 there is a shocking debilitation in his work. The symptoms of it are plain too: a flat and moralistic and not often very passionate adaptation of Christian and classical vocabularies; a tendency to increased garrulity; a soberly cheery optimism about the relations of man and nature, man and God, combined with a sort of peevishness against railroads and a zeal for capital punishment." Wordsworth himself had been aware of the dangers as early as 1800. In the Preface to the *Lyrical Ballads* he observes "a multitude of causes, unknown to former times, are now acting to blunt the discriminating powers of the mind . . . to reduce it to a state of almost savage torpor." He mentions "the great national events daily taking place," "the increasing accumulation of men in cities," and "the uniformity of their occupations."

One often reads lamentations on the elderly Wordsworth as a political reactionary, but the reasons that conservatism is so sad a falling-away from radical idealism are not made clear. They should be: the early Wordsworth gained, as we have seen, a moral authority from his visionary experience; radical idealism is simply one of several corollaries to that moral authority. His later political stance is significant far beyond the purely political sphere, for it shows the great diminution in the influence of his early vision on him.

In later life, commenting in a note to the poem on the ideas of the *Intimations of Immortality* ode, Wordsworth considered this change. In his youth, he says, he had been

> . . . often unable to think of earthly things as having external existence, and I communed with all that I saw as something not apart from, but inherent in, my own immaterial nature. Many times while going to school I have grasped at a wall or tree to recall myself from this abyss of idealism to the reality. At that time I was afraid of such processes. In later periods of life I have deplored, as we all have reason to do, a subjugation of an opposite character. . . .

He goes on to apologize, much as a Victorian professor might do, for the poem's having invited the inference by "good and pious persons" of his championing the idea of a prior state of existence. The idea, he concedes, is "not advanced in Revela-

tion," but "the Fall of Man presents an analogy in its favour."
It is "in the popular creeds of many nations" and "is known
as an ingredient in Platonic philosophy."

HOW CARLYLE CHANGED

A comparable loss of vision, if not of assertion, is true of Carlyle. He could not sustain the outlook of *Sartor Resartus*,[1] and
one does not have to thumb the social history books to find
the forces which destroyed it. The first six chapters of the
work itself (appearing serially in 1833–34) concentrate on attacking those forces. From the opening pages, with their af-
fable irony at the expense of spiritless and over-specialized
research, occur a series of attacks: on the selfishness of business and industry; on exploitation of workers and the political system which encourages it; on excessive pragmatism;
on money-power; on misapplied technical "progress" ("The
first ground handful of Nitre, Sulphur, and Charcoal drove
Monk Schwartz's pestle through the ceiling: what will the
last do?"); on advertising ("puffery and quackery"); on popular newspapers; on the inactivity of the Church. As one follows Carlyle through his growing stress on hero-worship
(which had been in *Sartor* a mere corollary to his central
faith), through his idealizing of the Middle Ages in *Past and
Present*, he appears—differing from Wordsworth in this—to
lose even the consciousness of his former vision. Carlyle
sees democracy in *Past and Present* as the tired dragging
down of everything to the level of the meanest common de-
nominator: "Democracy, which means despair of finding
any Heroes to govern you, and contented putting up with the
want of them,—alas, thou too, mein Lieber, seest well how
close it is of kin to *Atheism*, and other sad Isms." There is no
reason to condemn a writer for preferring autocracy to
democracy; it is still an arguable matter, and the preference
in 1843, after decades of mob disturbances, probably appeared natural and sensible. What is sad here is not the position Carlyle takes, but the fact that the prophet alive with
faith has shrunk into political propagandist. Carlyle might
have seen himself that the *scope* of his concerns here,
slightly more than a decade after the assertive faith of *Sartor*, was very close of kin to agnosticism and other sad isms.
His attention is no longer on ideals, but on a social situation,

1. A work by Carlyle that combined a novel, essays, and autobiography

---

TRADITIONAL RELIGIOUS VIEWS IN ROMANTICISM
*Literary scholar and critic Northrop Frye explains the
conservative views, such as a belief in chivalry and tradi-*
tional Catholicism, that were held by Thomas Carlyle and
other Romantics.

In religion, many Romantics, especially on the Continent,
adopted a conservative or traditional Christian position, usually Roman Catholic, and saw in Romanticism a revival of an
age of faith, in reaction to the sterile enlightenment of the
eighteenth century, when a rational and analytic perspective
was thought to have reached an extreme. In British Romanticism, Edmund Burke, with his conception of a continuous social contract and his elegy over the passing of the age of
chivalry with the French Revolution, and [Thomas] Carlyle,
with his effort to reactivate the aristocracy and his vision of
the "organic filaments" of a new religion, represent this conservative tendency, along with the later religious writings of
Coleridge. It is still surviving in the historical nostalgia of the
early [William Butler] Yeats and in the various mythical con-
structs which show us Western culture as having steadily declined since the Middle Ages, a historical fall being sometimes
associated with a certain phase which the mythologist particularly dislikes, such as the Reformation, the philosophy of
[Francis] Bacon, the secularism of the Renaissance, "usura"
(Pound), or "dissociation of sensibility" (Eliot).

Northrop Frye, *A Study of English Romanticism.* New York: Random House, 1968.

---

the lack of "hero" material. Raymond Williams, who sees
Carlyle's shift as moving from a real insight predicated on
human needs to the substitution of what he (Carlyle) desired
personally, comments, "The phenomenon is indeed general,
and has perhaps been especially marked in the last six or
seven generations." He goes on to describe the process:

> This indeed is the tragedy of the situation: that a genuine in-
> sight, a genuine vision, should be dragged down by the very
> situation, the very structure of relationships, to which it was
> opposed, until a civilizing insight became in its operation
> barbarous, and a heroic purpose, a 'high vocation', found its
> final expression in a conception of human relationships
> which is only an idealized version of industrial class-society.

A sense of the withdrawal from Romantic attitudes is
perhaps most succinctly suggested by various hints drawn
from nineteenth century literature as a whole. Professor
Walter Houghton suggests that love of woman, as expressed

in [Coventry] Patmore's *The Angel in the House,* was one substitute for certainty of belief. Or if we put the kind of duty we associate with [Rudyard] Kipling beside the kind Carlyle speaks of in *Sartor,* it is hard to avoid the impression that Kipling's is an isolated vestigial survival. Or again, Wordsworth had used "forms" to express his vision, but later in the century their significance dwindles. . . . For [Matthew] Arnold natural forms are the inscrutable symbols of a lonely, remote and inexorable existence, essentially fruitless clues in a dispiriting puzzle. For [John] Ruskin they were initially what they had been for Wordsworth, the language of moral guidance spoken by God; but as Ruskin develops they are more often seen only as background to human diminution or repression of spirit, and their main level of meaning becomes social. The logical conclusion of this general loss of significance comes in the eighties and nineties, where the sensual experience of the form entirely dominates the artist's interest, and the contrast with Romanticism becomes complete.

"Disorder," Carlyle once wrote, "is dissolution, death. No chaos but it seeks a centre to revolve round." He was at the time pleading the case for hero-worship, but this itself was only the political expression of his need for faith, and for the return, in political clothes, of the Everlasting Yea.[2] We might recall, in moving to our own time, how far our most widely-read literary form, the novel, has been shaped round a parallel idea, though now "love" in various aspects is its main center. Judging by the number of twentieth century novels pleading for this, Matthew Arnold's brief and pathetic aside in *Dover Beach,* "Ah, love, let us be true to one another!" speaks for a whole legion of the lost.

---

2. A conversion narrative that is the final of the three books in *Sartor Resartus*

Romantic Poetry Is Aesthetically Trite

T.E. Hulme

T.E. Hulme explains why he dislikes Romantic poetry and hopes for a return to the classic style in the following viewpoint. According to Hulme, the core problem of Romantic poems is that they are overly emotional and whining. He is also critical of the Romantic fascination with the wild, unrestrained, and the infinite. To Hulme, the best poetry deals with small, ordinary things or situations that are familiar to many people. Hulme prefers poetry that adheres to the neoclassical style and its emphasis on the commonplace and definable, not the uncanny or unbelievable. Hulme was a critic and philosopher who helped found the school of Imagist poetry in the 1910s, which used precise visual images to achieve clarity of expression.

When I say that I dislike the romantics, I dissociate two things: the part of them in which they resemble all the great poets, and the part in which they differ and which gives them their character as romantics. It is this minor element which constitutes the particular note of a century, and which, while it excites contemporaries, annoys the next generation. It was precisely that quality in [Alexander] Pope which pleased his friends, which we detest. Now, anyone just before the romantics who felt that, could have predicted that a change was coming. It seems to me that we stand just in the same position now. I think that there is an increasing proportion of people who simply can't stand [Algernon] Swinburne.

When I say that there will be another classical revival I don't necessarily anticipate a return to Pope. I say merely that now is the time for such a revival. Given people of the necessary capacity, it may be a vital thing; without them we may

Excerpted from T.E. Hulme, *Speculations: Essays on Humanism and the Philosophy of Art* (London: Routledge & Kegan Paul Ltd., 1924).

get a formalism something like Pope. When it does come we may not even recognise it as classical. Although it will be classical it will be different because it has passed through a romantic period. To take a parallel example: I remember being very surprised, after seeing the Post Impressionists, to find in [French artist] Maurice Denis's account of the matter that they consider themselves classical in the sense that they were trying to impose the same order on the mere flux of new material provided by the impressionist movement, that existed in the more limited materials of the painting before.

A CRITICISM OF THE ROMANTICS

There is something now to be cleared away before I get on with my argument, which is that while romanticism is dead in reality, yet the critical attitude appropriate to it still continues to exist. To make this a little clearer: For every kind of verse, there is a corresponding receptive attitude. In a romantic period we demand from verse certain qualities. In a classical period we demand others. At the present time I should say that this receptive attitude has outlasted the thing from which it was formed. But while the romantic tradition has run dry, yet the critical attitude of mind, which demands romantic qualities from verse, still survives. So that if good classical verse were to be written to-morrow very few people would be able to stand it.

I object even to the best of the romantics. I object still more to the receptive attitude. I object to the sloppiness which doesn't consider that a poem is a poem unless it is moaning or whining about something or other. I always think in this connection of the last line of a poem of John Webster's which ends with a request I cordially endorse:

"End your moan and come away."

The thing has got so bad now that a poem which is all dry and hard, a properly classical poem, would not be considered poetry at all. How many people now can lay their hands on their hearts and say they like either Horace or Pope? They feel a kind of chill when they read them.

The dry hardness which you get in the classics is absolutely repugnant to them. Poetry that isn't damp isn't poetry at all. They cannot see that accurate description is a legitimate object of verse. Verse to them always means a bringing in of some of the emotions that are grouped round the word infinite.

THE RESULT OF ROMANTICISM

The essence of poetry to most people is that it must lead them to a beyond of some kind. Verse strictly confined to the earthly and the definite (Keats is full of it) might seem to them to be excellent writing, excellent craftsmanship, but not poetry. So much has romanticism debauched us, that, without some form of vagueness, we deny the highest.

In the classic it is always the light of ordinary day, never the light that never was on land or sea. It is always perfectly human and never exaggerated: man is always man and never a god.

But the awful result of romanticism is that, accustomed to this strange light, you can never live without it. Its effect on you is that of a drug.

There is a general tendency to think that verse means little else than the expression of unsatisfied emotion. People say: "But how can you have verse without sentiment?" You see what it is: the prospect alarms them. A classical revival to them would mean the prospect of an arid desert and the death of poetry as they understand it, and could only come to fill the gap caused by that death. Exactly why this dry classical spirit should have a positive and legitimate necessity to express itself in poetry is utterly inconceivable to them. . . .

JOHN RUSKIN'S VIEWS

It is an objection which ultimately I believe comes from a bad metaphysic of art. You are unable to admit the existence of beauty without the infinite being in some way or another dragged in.

I may quote for purposes of argument, as a typical example of this kind of attitude made vocal, the famous chapters in [John] Ruskin's *Modern Painters*, Vol. II, on the imagination. . . . I only use the word here because it is Ruskin's word. All that I am concerned with just now is the attitude behind it, which I take to be the romantic.

"Imagination cannot but be serious; she sees too far, too darkly, too solemnly, too earnestly, ever to smile. There is something in the heart of everything, if we can reach it, that we shall not be inclined to laugh at. . . . Those who have so pierced and seen the melancholy deeps of things, are filled with intense passion and gentleness of sympathy." (Part III, Chap. III, § 9.)

"There is in every word set down by the imaginative mind

an awful undercurrent of meaning, and evidence and shadow upon it of the deep places out of which it has come. It is often obscure, often half-told; for he who wrote it, in his clear seeing of the things beneath, may have been impatient of detailed interpretation; for if we choose to dwell upon it and trace it, it will lead us always securely back to that metropolis of the soul's dominion from which we may follow out all the ways and tracks to its farthest coasts." (Part III, Chap. III, § 5.)

Really in all these matters the act of judgment is an instinct, an absolutely unstateable thing akin to the art of the tea taster. But you must talk, and the only language you can use in this matter is that of analogy. I have no material clay to mould to the given shape; the only thing which one has for the purpose, and which acts as a substitute for it, a kind of mental clay, are certain metaphors modified into theories of æsthetic and rhetoric. A combination of these, while it cannot state the essentially unstateable intuition, can yet give you a sufficient analogy to enable you to see what it was and to recognise it on condition that you yourself have been in a similar state. Now these phrases of Ruskin's convey quite clearly to me his taste in the matter.

DEFINING BEAUTY

I see quite clearly that he thinks the best verse must be serious. That is a natural attitude for a man in the romantic period. But he is not content with saying that he prefers this kind of verse. He wants to deduce his opinion like his master, Coleridge, from some fixed principle which can be found by metaphysic.

Here is the last refuge of this romantic attitude. It proves itself to be not an attitude but a deduction from a fixed principle of the cosmos.

One of the main reasons for the existence of philosophy is not that it enables you to find truth (it can never do that) but that it does provide you a refuge for definitions. The usual idea of the thing is that it provides you with a fixed basis from which you can deduce the things you want in æsthetics. The process is the exact contrary. You start in the confusion of the fighting line, you retire from that just a little to the rear to recover, to get your weapons right. Quite plainly, without metaphor this—it provides you with an elaborate and precise language in which you really can explain definitely what you mean, but what you want to say is decided by other things. The ultimate reality is the hurly-burly, the struggle; the metaphysic is an adjunct to clear-headedness in it.

To get back to Ruskin and his objection to all that is not serious. It seems to me that involved in this is a bad metaphysical æsthetic. You have the metaphysic which in defining beauty or the nature of art always drags in the infinite. Particularly in Germany, the land where theories of æsthetics were first created, the romantic æsthetes collated all beauty to an impression of the infinite involved in the identification of our being in absolute spirit. In the least element of beauty we have a total intuition of the whole world. Every artist is a kind of pantheist.

Now it is quite obvious to anyone who holds this kind of theory that any poetry which confines itself to the finite can never be of the highest kind. It seems a contradiction in terms to them. And as in metaphysics you get the last refuge of a prejudice, so it is now necessary for me to refute this.

Here follows a tedious piece of dialectic, but it is necessary for my purpose. I must avoid two pitfalls in discussing the idea of beauty. On the one hand there is the old classical view which is supposed to define it as lying in conformity to certain standard fixed forms ; and on the other hand there is the romantic view which drags in the infinite. I have got to find a metaphysic between these two which will enable me to hold consistently that a neo-classic[1] verse of the type I have indicated involves no contradiction in terms. It is essential to prove that beauty may be in small, dry things.

THE STRUGGLE OF ARTISTRY

The great aim is accurate, precise and definite description. The first thing is to recognise how extraordinarily difficult this is. It is no mere matter of carefulness; you have to use language, and language is by its very nature a communal thing; that is, it expresses never the exact thing but a compromise—that which is common to you, me and everybody. But each man sees a little differently, and to get out clearly and exactly what he does see, he must have a terrific struggle with language, whether it be with words or the technique of other arts. Language has its own special nature, its

---

1. Referring to neo-classicism, which was the dominant literary movement in England from 1660 till 1778, when Romanticism supplanted it. Neo-classicism emphasized restraint, decorum, and logic.

own conventions and communal ideas. It is only by a concentrated effort of the mind that you can hold it fixed to your own purpose. I always think that the fundamental process at the back of all the arts might be represented by the following metaphor. You know what I call architect's curves—flat pieces of wood with all different kinds of curvature. By a suitable selection from these you can draw approximately any curve you like. The artist I take to be the man who simply can't bear the idea of that 'approximately.' He will get the exact curve of what he sees whether it be an object or an idea in the mind. I shall here have to change my metaphor a little to get the process in his mind. Suppose that instead of your curved pieces of wood you have a springy piece of steel of the same types of curvature as the wood. Now the state of tension or concentration of mind, if he is doing anything really good in this struggle against the ingrained habit of the technique, may be represented by a man employing all his fingers to bend the steel out of its own curve and into the exact curve which you want. Something different to what it would assume naturally.

There are then two things to distinguish, first the particular faculty of mind to see things as they really are, and apart from the conventional ways in which you have been trained to see them. This is itself rare enough in all consciousness. Second, the concentrated state of mind, the grip over oneself which is necessary in the actual expression of what one sees. To prevent one falling into the conventional curves of ingrained technique, to hold on through infinite detail and trouble to the exact curve you want. Wherever you get this sincerity, you get the fundamental quality of good art without dragging in infinite or serious.

I can now get at that positive fundamental quality of verse which constitutes excellence, which has nothing to do with infinity, with mystery or with emotions.

This is the point I aim at, then, in my argument. I prophesy that a period of dry, hard, classical verse is coming. I have met the preliminary objection founded on the bad romantic æsthetic that in such verse, from which the infinite is excluded, you cannot have the essence of poetry at all.

Chronology

1756

Novelist and political writer, also the father of Mary Shelley, William Godwin is born.

1757

Poet and artist William Blake is born.

1759

Writer and women's rights advocate Mary Wollstonecraft is born.

1760

King George II dies, succeeded by his grandson, who becomes King George III.

1770

Poet William Wordsworth is born.

1771

Poet and novelist Walter Scott is born.

1772

Poet Samuel Taylor Coleridge is born.

1774

Poet Robert Southey is born.

1775

The American War for Independence begins at the Battle of Lexington; novelist Jane Austen is born; essayist Charles Lamb is born.

1776

American Congress passes the *Declaration of Independence*; historian Edward Gibbons publishes *Decline and Fall of the Roman Empire*; economist Adam Smith publishes *Wealth of Nations.*

1778

Essayist William Hazlitt is born.

1781

British troops surrender to Americans at Yorktown.

1788

Poet George Gordon (Lord) Byron is born; George III has his first attack of "madness," brought on by porphyria.

1789

The French Revolution begins; Blake writes *Songs of Innocence* and *The Book of Thel.*

1791

Political philosopher Thomas Paine publishes *Rights of Man.*

1792

Poet Percy Bysshe Shelley is born; Wollstonecraft publishes *Vindication of the Rights of Women.*

1794

Blake writes *Songs of Experience.*

1795

Poet John Keats is born; poet Thomas Carlyle is born.

1796

Coleridge writes *The Eolian Harp.*

1797

Novelist Mary Wollstonecraft Godwin, daughter of William Godwin and Mary Wollstonecraft is born; Wollstonecraft dies ten days after giving birth; Blake writes "The Four Zoas"; Coleridge writes "Kubla Khan."

1798

Coleridge writes "The Ancient Mariner" and "Frost at Midnight"; Wordsworth and Coleridge publish *Lyrical Ballads*; Wordsworth writes "Lines Composed a Few Miles Above Tintern Abbey."

1801

Scott writes *Ballads.*

1802

Coleridge writes "Dejection: An Ode."

1803

Britain declares war on France.

1804–1808

Blake writes "Milton."

1804–1820

Blake writes "Jerusalem."

1805

Naval commander Horatio Nelson leads England to victory over France and Spain at the Battle of Trafalgar but dies in the process; Scott writes "The Lay of the Last Minstrel"; Wordsworth writes "The Prelude."

1807

Wordsworth publishes *Poems.*

1810

Scott writes *The Lady of the Lake.*

1811

King George III's illness leads to him being declared insane and his son, the Prince of Wales, becoming Regent; Austen publishes *Sense and Sensibility;* Lamb writes *On the Tragedies of Shakespeare.*

1812

British prime minister Spencer Perceval is assassinated in the House of Commons; United States declares war on Britain; Byron writes "Childe Harold Cantos I and II"; Southey is named Poet Laureate of England after Scott declines the honor.

1813

Austen's *Pride and Prejudice* is published; Shelley writes "Queen Mab."

1813–1814

Byron writes "The Giaour" and "The Corsair."

1814

British forces burn the District of Columbia; Treaty of Ghent ends the War of 1812; Wordsworth writes "The Excursion"; Austen publishes *Mansfield Park;* Shelley and Mary Godwin meet and elope; Scott publishes *Waverley.*

1815

French military leader Napoleon is defeated at Waterloo.

1816

Coleridge publishes "Christabel" and "Kubla Khan"; Byron writes "Childe Harold Cantos III and IV"; Shelley writes "Alastor"; Shelley and Mary Godwin wed following the suicide of his wife, Harriet Westbrook; Austen publishes *Emma.*

1817

Austen dies; Coleridge's *Biographia Literaria* is published; Hazlitt writes *Characters of Shakspeare's Plays;* Mary Shelley writes *Frankenstein, or the Modern Prometheus;* Byron writes "Manfred"; Keats writes *Poems,* which includes "Sleep and Poetry" and "On First Looking into Chapman's Homer."

1818

Austen's *Northanger Abbey* and *Persuasion* are published posthumously; Keats writes "Endymion"; Scott writes *Heart of Midlothian* and *Rob Roy.*

1818–1824

Byron writes *Don Juan.*

1819

The future queen, Victoria, is born; Keats writes "The Fall of Hyperion."

1820

King George III dies, succeeded by his son the Prince Regent, who becomes King George IV; Shelley writes "The Cenci" and "Prometheus Unbound"; Scott writes *Ivanhoe;* Keats publishes *Lamia, Isabella, The Eve of St. Agnes, and Other Poems.*

1821

Keats dies in Rome of tuberculosis; Shelley writes "Adonais" in Keats's honor; Shelley writes "A Defense of Poetry"; Byron writes "Cain"; Thomas de Quincey writes *Confessions of an English Opium-Eater.*

1822

Shelley dies; Lamb writes "A Dissertation Upon Roast Pig"; Byron writes "The Vision of Judgment."

1824

Byron dies at Missolonghi, Greece; Shelley's *Posthumous Poems* is published.

1825

Hazlitt writes *Spirit of the Age.*

1826

Hazlitt writes *The Plain Speaker*; Mary Shelley writes *The Last Man.*

1827

Blake dies.

1828

Scott writes *The Fair Maid of Perth*; Leigh Hunt writes *Lord Byron and Some of His Contemporaries.*

1830

King George IV dies, succeeded by his brother, who becomes King William IV; Hazlitt dies.

1833–1834

Carlyle writes *Sartor Resartus.*

1834

Coleridge and Lamb die.

1835

Wordsworth publishes *Yarrow Revisited and Other Poems* and "On the Power of Sound"; Mary Shelley writes "Lodore."

1836

William Godwin dies.

1837

Victoria becomes queen of England after her uncle, King William IV, dies childless.

1838

Carlyle writes *Sir Walter Scott.*

1843

Southey dies.

1850

Wordsworth dies; his poem *The Prelude* is published posthumously.

1851

Mary Shelley dies.

1881

Carlyle dies.

FOR FURTHER RESEARCH

ABOUT ENGLISH ROMANTICS

M.H. Abrams, *The Correspondent Breeze: Essays on English Romanticism.* New York: W.W. Norton, 1984.

Patricia M. Adair, *The Waking Dream: A Study of Coleridge's Poetry.* London: Edward Arnold, 1967.

Meena Alexander, *Women in Romanticism: Mary Wollstonecraft, Dorothy Wordsworth, and Mary Shelley.* Savage, MD: Barnes & Noble, 1989.

Carlos Baker, *Shelley's Major Poetry: The Fabric of a Vision.* New York: Russell & Russell, 1961.

John Beer, *Romantic Influences: Contemporary, Victorian, Modern.* New York: St. Martin's, 1993.

Ernest Bernbaum, *Guide Through the Romantic Movement.* New York: Ronald, 1949.

Harold Bloom, *The Visionary Company: A Reading of English Romantic Poetry.* Ithaca, NY: Cornell University Press, 1971.

Harold Bloom, ed., *William Hazlitt.* New York: Chelsea House, 1986.

Crane Brinton, *The Political Ideas of the English Romanticists.* New York: Russell & Russell, 1962.

Derek Colville, *Victorian Poetry and the Romantic Religion.* Albany: State University of New York Press, 1970.

Heather Coombs, *Authors in Their Age: The Age of Keats and Shelley.* London: Blackie, 1978.

R.T. Davies and B.G. Beatty, eds., *Literature of the Romantic Period, 1750–1850.* Liverpool: Liverpool University Press, 1976.

Margaret Drabble, *Literature in Perspective: Wordsworth.* London: Evans Brothers, 1966.

June Dwyer, *Jane Austen.* New York: Continuum, 1989.

James Engell, *The Creative Imagination: Enlightenment to Romanticism.* Cambridge, MA: Harvard University Press, 1981.

Hoxie Neal Fairchild, *Religious Trends in English Poetry: Volume III.* New York: Columbia University Press, 1949.

Northrop Frye, *A Study of English Romanticism.* New York: Random House, 1968.

Lilian R. Furst, *Romanticism in Perspective.* London: Macmillan, 1969.

D.G. Gillham, *William Blake.* London: Cambridge University Press, 1973.

Richard Gravil, Lucy Newlyn, and Nicholas Roe, eds., *Coleridge's Imagination: Essays in Memory of Pete Laver.* London: Cambridge University Press, 1985.

C.H. Herford, *The Age of Wordsworth.* London: George Bell, 1897.

David Gwilym James, *Matthew Arnold and the Decline of English Romanticism.* Oxford: Clarendon, 1961.

Paul Magnuson, *Coleridge and Wordsworth: A Lyrical Dialogue.* Princeton, NJ: Princeton University Press, 1988.

Leslie A. Marchand, *Byron's Poetry: A Critical Introduction.* Boston: Houghton Mifflin, 1965.

Robin Mayhead, *Walter Scott.* London: Cambridge University Press, 1973.

Thomas McFarland, *Romantic Cruxes: The English Essayists and the Spirit of the Age.* Oxford: Clarendon, 1987.

Anne K. Mellor, *Mary Shelley: Her Life, Her Fiction, Her Monsters.* New York: Methuen, 1988.

Anne K. Mellor, ed., *Romanticism and Feminism.* Bloomington: Indiana University Press, 1988.

Michael Phillips, ed., *Interpreting Blake: Essays.* Cambridge, England: Cambridge University Press, 1978.

H.W. Piper, *The Active Universe: Pantheism and the Concept of Imagination in the English Romantic Poets.* London: Athlone, 1962.

James Pipkin, ed., *English and German Romanticism: Cross-Currents and Controversies.* Heidelberg: Carl Winter Universitätsverlag, 1985.

Eino Railo, *The Haunted Castle: A Study of the Elements of English Romanticism.* New York: Humanities, 1964.

George Barnett Smith, *Shelley: A Critical Biography.* New York: Haskell House, 1974.

Muriel Spark, *Mary Shelley.* London: Constable, 1987.

Stuart M. Sperry, *Keats the Poet.* Princeton, NJ: Princeton University Press, 1973.

Anya Taylor, *Magic and English Romanticism.* Athens: University of Georgia Press, 1979.

Clarence De Witt Thorpe, *The Mind of John Keats.* New York: Russell & Russell, 1964.

William Walsh, *Coleridge: The Work and the Relevance.* London: Chatto & Windus, 1967.

About the Romantic Era

John W. Derry, *Reaction and Reform, 1793–1868: England in the Early Nineteenth Century.* London: Blandford, 1963.

A.F. Fremantle, *England in the Nineteenth Century.* Millwood, NY: Kraus Reprint, 1978.

William Gibson, *Church, State, and Society, 1760–1850.* New York: St. Martin's, 1994.

R.B. Mowat, *The Romantic Age: Europe in the Early Nineteenth Century.* London: George G. Harrap, 1937.

John Plowright, *Regency England: The Age of Lord Liverpool.* London: Routledge, 1996.

J.H. Plumb, *England in the Eighteenth Century.* Baltimore: Penguin, 1963.

Michael Reed, *The Georgian Triumph, 1700–1830.* London: Routledge and Kegan Paul, 1983.

George Macaulay Trevelyan, *British History in the Nineteenth Century (1782–1901).* New York: Longmans, Green, 1922.

William B. Wilcox and Walter L. Arnstein, *The Age of Aristocracy: 1688 to 1830.* Lexington, MA: D.C. Heath, 1983.

INDEX